# HIS, HERS, THEIRS

## ABOUT THE AUTHOR

Tobe Aleksander is a writer and broadcaster on a wide range of consumer, legal and financial issues. As a professional adviser she worked with the Citizen's Advice Bureau. She also teaches assertiveness and communication skills. Her books include *Assertive Consumer: An Everyday Guide to Your Rights at Home, Work and in the High Street* (1990); *The Complete Guide to Living Together* (1992); *The Right to be Yourself* (1992); *Separation and Divorce: A Guide for Women in Mid-life and Beyond* (1995). Tobe lives in London with her lawyer husband and their two cats.

This book is a guide, written in general terms to be accessible to a wide readership. In addition, laws and practices may change. While all reasonable care has been taken in preparing the information contained in this book, neither the author nor the publisher accepts responsibility for any errors it may contain or for any loss, however caused from reliance on it.

# HIS, HERS, THEIRS
# A FINANCIAL HANDBOOK FOR STEPFAMILIES

Tobe Aleksander

Published by

STEPFAMILY PUBLICATIONS
National Stepfamily Association

First published in Great Britain
by STEPFAMILY Publications in 1995

National Stepfamily Association
Chapel House 18 Hatton Place
London EC1N 8RU

Registered Charity No 1005351

Company Limited by guarantee No 2552166

Telephone: 0171 209 2460 (office)
             0171 209 2464 (Counselling line)

ISBN 1 873309 13 9

Edited and indexed by Sally Lansdell Yeung
Printed by Blackfords of Cornwall
Designed by Ravenscourt Design Partnership, London W6
Illustrations by Sweety & Squid

# NATWEST UK COMMUNITY INVESTMENT

The ability to make informed judgements regarding the use and management of money is a critical life skill, and crucial to our business. NatWest UK has focused its Community Investment Programme on the development of understanding personal money management and enterprise skills for individuals and organisations.

Through its Community Investment Programme, NatWest UK aims to make a difference to the communities in which it operates. By supporting carefully managed initiatives, often working alongside others, benefit is gained by all those involved. The proposal for a book to help financial planning seemed a good project for NatWest UK support during the International Year of the Family and we are pleased to have worked with our sponsorship partners, the National Stepfamily Association.

Money can, at times, be a tricky subject to deal with and this is all the more so when families are disrupted, disadvantaged or under stress. At the time of separation and divorce, money management is a difficult issue with practical and emotional consequences.

Helping to improve the availability and quality of money advice provided by independent advice services is an area where NatWest UK has an established track record. For many years we have supported independent money advisors such as Citizens Advice Bureaux workers, to whom so many people go for help and we are pleased that this book will complement these busy advice services.

The number of people living in stepfamilies is a startling one, many of whom are, no doubt, NatWest customers: over 2 million children and young people, each with two parents and many with two step-parents, and added to that there are often four sets of grandparents and step-grandparents! The implications for financial planning are enormous. This book helps to explain the issues and establish a clear path through the money management maze.

NatWest UK is delighted to sponsor this book.

Julia Fell
*Head of Community Investment*
NatWest UK

# CONTENTS

## PART THREE: THE FINANCIAL ESSENTIALS

## PART FOUR:
## EXTRA HELP AND INFORMATION

# ACKNOWLEDGEMENTS

A great number of people have been involved in the thinking, planning and production of this book. The Vice Chair of the National Stepfamily Association, Barrie Irving, raised the issue of financial planning many years ago, based not only on his own experience of the need for more specialised information but also because as a telephone counsellor he was aware that many callers were struggling with money issues which needed more than a sympathetic counselling ear to help them and their different stepfamily members.

We were delighted when NatWest UK very generously agreed to sponsor this financial planning project as part of their contribution to the International Year of the Family.

Many of our telephone counsellors, local groups and contacts, and our Trustees contributed their thoughts and experiences on both the need for, and often the lack of, appropriate financial planning advice to meet the very different needs of stepfamilies as they form, develop and change.

We are particularly indebted to two of our Trustees who read through the first draft and provided useful additional insights. We also want to thank those who read the manuscript with an expert eye from their own professional perspective: Emma Knights and Alison Garnham, from CPAG (Child Poverty Action Group); Wendy Mantle, Family Solicitor; and John Taylor, of the Independent Financial Advisers Barney Wilkins & Howard Ltd. Finally, of course, our thanks go to our sponsors who made the whole exercise possible.

It is the intention of NatWest UK that a copy of this book should be made available to every Citizen's Advice Bureau and each NatWest branch to ensure that information on this particular area of family finance is widely available both to advisers and to their clients and customers.

By its very nature some of the information in this book will alter as revisions and additions are introduced in areas such as child support, divorce law, pension regulations and other aspects of welfare payments, family law and financial regulation.

**Please remember that this is not a do-it-yourself book but a guide to some of the areas you need to think about, questions you need to ask, information you need to record, and ways of dealing with money matters. Do always seek professional legal or financial advice.**

# Stepfamily relationships

**MEN** (columns) × **WOMEN** (rows)

| WOMEN \ MEN | SINGLE — NO CHILDREN | SINGLE — RESIDENT CHILDREN | SINGLE — NON RESIDENT CHILDREN | WIDOWER — NO CHILDREN | WIDOWER — RESIDENT CHILDREN | WIDOWER — NON RESIDENT CHILDREN | DIVORCED/SEPARATED — NO CHILDREN | DIVORCED/SEPARATED — RESIDENT CHILDREN | DIVORCED/SEPARATED — NON RESIDENT CHILDREN |
|---|---|---|---|---|---|---|---|---|---|
| **SINGLE — NO CHILDREN** | | 1 | 2 PART-TIME | | 3 | 4 PART-TIME | | 5 | 6 PART-TIME |
| **SINGLE — RESIDENT CHILDREN** | 7 | 8 STEP-SIBLINGS | 9 STEP-SIBLINGS | 10 | 11 STEP-SIBLINGS | 12 STEP-SIBLINGS | 13 | 14 STEP-SIBLINGS | 15 STEP-SIBLINGS |
| **SINGLE — NON RESIDENT CHILDREN** | 16 PART-TIME | 17 STEP-SIBLINGS | 18 PART-TIME STEP-SIBLINGS | 19 PART-TIME | 20 STEP-SIBLINGS | 21 PART-TIME STEP-SIBLINGS | 22 PART-TIME | 23 STEP-SIBLINGS | 24 PART-TIME STEP-SIBLINGS |
| **WIDOW — NO CHILDREN** | | 25 | 26 PART-TIME | | 27 | 28 PART-TIME | | 29 | 30 PART-TIME |
| **WIDOW — RESIDENT CHILDREN** | 31 | 32 STEP-SIBLINGS | 33 STEP-SIBLINGS | 34 | 35 STEP-SIBLINGS | 36 STEP-SIBLINGS | 37 | 38 STEP-SIBLINGS | 39 STEP-SIBLINGS |
| **WIDOW — NON RESIDENT CHILDREN** | 40 PART-TIME | 41 STEP-SIBLINGS | 42 PART-TIME STEP-SIBLINGS | 43 PART-TIME | 44 STEP-SIBLINGS | 45 PART-TIME STEP-SIBLINGS | 46 PART-TIME | 47 STEP-SIBLINGS | 48 PART-TIME STEP-SIBLINGS |
| **DIVORCED/SEPARATED — NO CHILDREN** | | 49 | 50 PART-TIME | | 51 | 52 PART-TIME | | 53 | 54 PART-TIME |
| **DIVORCED/SEPARATED — RESIDENT CHILDREN** | 55 | 56 STEP-SIBLINGS | 57 STEP-SIBLINGS | 58 | 59 STEP-SIBLINGS | 60 STEP-SIBLINGS | 61 | 62 STEP-SIBLINGS | 63 STEP-SIBLINGS |
| **DIVORCED/SEPARATED — NON RESIDENT CHILDREN** | 64 PART-TIME | 65 STEP-SIBLINGS | 66 PART-TIME STEP-SIBLINGS | 67 PART-TIME | 68 STEP-SIBLINGS | 69 PART-TIME STEP-SIBLINGS | 70 PART-TIME | 71 STEP-SIBLINGS | 72 PART-TIME STEP-SIBLINGS |

# FOREWORD

Stepfamilies are not new. Over 150 years ago many stepchildren worried about who would feed, clothe and house them and what would become of their inheritance after the death of one parent and the remarriage of the other. In 1995 we worry more about how to make money stretch across two, often three and sometimes four or more families after one or both parents has repartnered or remarried.

## What is a stepfamily?

A stepfamily is created when two adults form a new household in which one or both brings a child or children from a previous relationship.

Stepfamilies can be very hard to understand because by their very formation they are enormously diverse and complex. There are at least 72 different ways of becoming a stepfamily (see the diagram opposite), because the two people moving into the new partnerships may have had very different experiences prior to their relationship. Such families may be preceded by single parenthood, separation, divorce or bereavement and may arise through cohabitation, marriage or remarriage. Stepchildren may be full-time or part-time members of the household according to which stepfamily they spend most of their time with. Stepfamily relationships cut across all generations. Many adults who are step-parents through their own new relationships may also become stepchildren as many of the older generation remarry. This is leading to an increasingly varied and complex network of stepfamily relationships.

In the diagram of the different kinds of stepfamilies, we have indicated past marital status but not current, that is whether the step-couple are cohabiting or married, because it would just become too complicated. It does mean, however, that you really do need to work out what kind of stepfamily you are if you are thinking of giving or taking advice from others who may not be aware of all the different possibilities and permutations.

## How many stepfamilies are there?

Around one in eight children is likely to grow up in a stepfamily. Currently one in five children is in a lone parent family and within five years of separation and divorce over half those mothers and fathers have remarried or repartnered. Over one million children were growing up in a full-time stepfamily in 1991 in Great Britain (Haskey, 1994) with a similar number in part-time stepfamilies, when they visit at weekends or holidays. The pressures on stepfamilies are many and varied, but in all the literature, the research and from our counselling calls there is one clear message that the biggest difficulties are around money and children.

---

*"When you create a stepfamily accept that all this is new and everything which went before – rules, discipline, money – is up for renegotiation. Above all talk about everything and anything and keep a sense of humour."*

---

Stepfamily households can vary in several ways. In addition to the ways in which stepfamilies are formed they then develop their own family formation – over half of all full-time stepfamilies have at least one joint child of their own.

---

*"Don't expect things in your new stepfamily to be the same as your previous relationship. Relax and let the relationship develop – give it time."*

---

To simplify matters, let's stay with the six main types of stepfamilies (see diagram opposite) just based on the three key facts of:

- whether either of the couple has a child,
- whether any of the children live with them, and
- whether they have their own child.

Who has children and where they live are important in working out child support according to the new Child Support Act formula.

As many stepfamilies will tell you, life in a stepfamily may vary from week to week or month to month. Trying to plan and make sense of what is happening, where and with whom, can therefore be more difficult if children spend different periods of time in different households – perhaps a week with Mum and then a week with Dad. As children get older they may decide they want to go and live with their other parent, so we cannot assume that brothers and sisters will all stay together in the same house. This can cause disruption to any attempt at financial planning when the child support goes to one house and the child is in another.

# What kind of stepfamily are you?

## Why are money matters for stepfamilies any different to other families?

Money matters are often a headache for any couple or family. The difficulties for stepfamilies arise because there is often more than one couple involved, more than one family. The financial inter-dependency, where money comes into a stepfamily for stepchildren and money goes out to stepsiblings elsewhere, rarely goes equally or smoothly. A late payment from one ex-partner and non-residential parent can create financial problems for another. Their payments to another stepfamily, also as ex-partner and non-residential parent, may then be delayed, and so it may go on if each family receiving child support has a similar chain of commitments.

If just one parent loses a job, takes a cut in salary, has reduced overtime or increased work costs or family responsibilities, the knock-on effect can involve many children and the adults looking after them.

---

*"As with any relationship be honest and open with each other about finances and involve the children – it minimises the jealousy."*

---

People who remarry or repartner usually face different financial considerations to those they faced the first time round.

- The couple is usually less well off. The General Household Survey 1991 (1993) noted that stepfamilies were better off than lone parent households with dependent children, but worse off than two parent traditional family households.

- Stepfamily couples often start off with a greater disparity and inequality in what they bring into the household. Unlike young newly weds who may be equally broke or both set up with careers and independent accommodation, a lone or non-resident parent is more likely to have a different range of assets, debts and liabilities resulting from their past.

- Stepfamily couples may be unequal before the law because they are cohabiting rather than married, or because, although a step-parent is not liable for assessment from the Child Support Agency and gets no recognition in his or her exempt or protected income for any expenses connected with any stepchildren, stepchildren can still go to court for child support if they have been treated as a 'child of the family'.

## Are there differences in the way people handle money in stepfamilies?

Very little has been written on this subject. Although there is some research on family obligations and income this has tended to concentrate on the cost of care of elderly relatives, differences between men and women and how money is allocated within the family.

However, an American book on remarriage and your money (Estess, 1992) describes five money stages that most remarrieds go through.

The Rose-Coloured Glasses stage – that romantic period when love seems capable of conquering everything, so you assume that there will be no money conflicts or that your love will give you the strength to overcome all obstacles:

> *"I knew he already had an ex-wife and two children to support, but we were so much in love that it didn't seem possible that anything as mundane as money could be a problem for us."*

The Don't-Rock-the-Boat stage – when feelings of resentment and anger start to surface as you find out your partner's approach to money is different (they spend too much or too little, on the wrong things, or without consulting you), or one or both of your ex-partners start to delay payments, or demand more, but you don't want to voice your feelings in case this puts pressure on your relationship and creates rows and conflict between you both:

> *"I can't believe how annoyed I get each month when I see him writing out this enormous cheque to his ex-wife and then he spends more money when the children come over to visit every other weekend. Obviously he wants to give them treats when they visit us and they are very friendly children and I enjoy seeing them."*

The Lay-it-on-the-Table stage – when you finally can't stand it anymore you have to express your concerns, voice your anger, be honest about what you want, argue about priorities, and speak openly about your fears, feelings and frustrations over money:

*"By the end of the first year I could feel the anger building up inside me. I realised that we had not talked about having our own child for some months, that I didn't want to have to keep on working but was getting frightened that we would not be able to afford to have a baby and to maintain our standard of living if he kept on spending so much on his first family."*

The Getting-it-Together stage – the stepcouple work out a mutually agreed way of handling finances and making financial decisions. It doesn't necessarily mean that money matters are any easier but that they are clearer, and discussed, and agreed, and reviewed regularly. They try and work out who does what best in terms of handling the accounts, drawing up the budgets and checking they stay within their agreements.

Sometimes this leads to a stepcouple having their own separate accounts and one joint account. Working out what comes out of which account provides the opportunity to discuss whose income is being used, who and what it is for, check the amount is appropriate and try and sort out any uncomfortable feelings.

| His Income | Her Income |
|---|---|
| Salary, overtime, investments, gifts, windfalls | Salary, child support from ex-partner, investments, gifts, windfalls |

**FAMILY ACCOUNTS**

Rent/mortgage, council tax, house insurance
Household expenses
Food
Expenses for their joint children
Family holidays and entertainment
Savings for emergencies and planned items

| His Accounts | Her Accounts |
|---|---|
| Spousal maintenance | Pension |
| Child support | Life insurance |
| Fares for children to visit | Fares for children to visit grandparents |
| Pension | Health insurance policy |
| Life insurance | Gifts for her children/family |
| Health insurance policy | Clothes |
| Gifts for his children/family | Personal expenses |
| Personal expenses | Car |
| Clothes | Hobbies/leisure activities |
| Cars | Savings for her children |
| Hobbies/leisure activities | Joint fund for family accounts |
| Savings for his children | |
| Joint fund for family accounts | |

The Achieving-Stability stage – by now the stepcouple really have control of their finances and feel they are able to make and take decisions jointly without either one feeling neglected or used. Often by the time you have reached this stage the children have ceased to be so totally dependent, money is less stretched and the stepcouple are able to use the practice over the years to settle new issues that will arise, such as paying for a child's wedding or re-assessing their wills and inheritance matters.

---

*"In the early days of our marriage arguments over money seemed to dominate our every waking hour. My stepchildren wanted expensive trainers and holidays on top of the child support we were already paying, my children wanted bikes and their father was always behind with the child support, and with two new babies I just wanted a new washing machine. Now that they have nearly all left home I can't believe the difference it makes not always having to worry about whether you will make it to the end of the month without over-spending. Mind you, with two of them getting married next year – his daughter and mine, it looks as though we shall be scrimping and saving again for a while."*

---

Clearly the emotional experiences we bring to any relationship will shape our attitude and response to money matters. There are some exercises in the book to help you identify what your emotional style may be and how that may be different to your new partner's.

---

*"Stepfamilies should sit down and discuss every aspect of their relationship. Communicate openly with each other. Don't stop talking until as many agreements or compromises have been reached as possible. Share the basis of your agreements with children but try and maintain child/adult boundaries in discussions about finances."*

---

## Outside forces that affect stepfamilies

Money matters in stepfamilies are also shaped by legislation, which has not kept pace with the changing forms and responsibilities of stepfamily life. It would be insensitive to think that we could counsel ourselves to be better money managers when some aspects of financial planning are beyond our control.

The Child Support Act, for example, has left many stepfathers feeling that they are expected to pay three times over – the capital sum they agreed at the time of their original divorce settlement, the new child support assessment, and the continued financial responsibilities for their stepchildren where their own father is unavailable or unable to support them. It also makes assumptions about the priority you must give to different financial payments. In our list of family accounts above, the child support payments would certainly be expected to come before pension, health care policy, fares for children to visit you or a car, no matter whether your pension was a mandatory payment, the car essential to get to work and you were determined to remain a significant and active parent to your children who were living apart from you.

## How to use this book

This book is not a do-it-yourself or definitive guide to financial wizardry and certainly can't help one average income accommodate the needs of several families. It is designed to help you understand some of the feelings behind money matters, to alleviate some of the tension before you get down to exploring the options for you at this stage of family transitions, and to assist you in working out the questions you need to ask of yourself, your partner and those from whom you seek help and advice. Much of the information for stepfamilies is exactly the same for all other families, but there is an extra or added component to consider. This book is designed to help you identify what that extra component is and how it might affect your options and your decisions.

For example, over half (52%) of all full-time stepfamilies have their own child. Some stepfamilies limit themselves to one child because they feel they cannot afford any more, others decide they cannot afford a child at all. While money is part of the decision-making process there are clearly many other issues to take into account.

Making a will is something that many of us put off. In a step-family, because inheritance is through the blood line, it is essential to make a will if you want your stepchildren to inherit from a step-parent's estate. How you do that can vary and because of the extra stepfamily component the wording and intention needs to be spelled out in great detail. Being aware of the differences and problems can help you work out what you don't want to happen as well as what you do want.

Appointing a guardian for all your children is important in case anything happens to one or both of you. But appointing a guardian without making financial provision could put an impossible burden on the named person(s) who may end up not able to look after your children after all.

Finally, do remember that throughout any family's life there may be unexpected changes. Stepfamilies are different, mainly in that they are likely to experience more change, more often and be more vulnerable to changes in other people's lives as well. Do seek advice at any and every stage of stepfamily life where you need to review and plan your finances. We are only too aware that most professionals in the whole sphere of welfare, education, social, psychological, legal and financial matters are not given any training or information on the differences for stepfamilies. Do always seek a member of the Solicitors' Family Law Association (SFLA) for advice on family legal matters (see page 180).

Always ask anyone you turn to for advice precisely how they think that the differences in your needs as a stepfamily are accounted for, and take with you the suggested questions we raise throughout this book. Your adviser may not know the answer, and you may like to reassure them that you know this is a complex area, but you would like them to find out and let you have a written statement on how the differences are taken account of, as well as the advantages and disadvantages open to you as options for financial planning.

As we have been at pains to point out, stepfamilies are very different and there is no readymade easy answer to most of the questions that will be in your mind. What you need to do is work out what your situation is – what type of stepfamily you are, what commitments you have, what financial resources you have available and how you can make the most effective and efficient use of them for the satisfaction of those concerned.

---

*"If you're thinking of becoming a stepfamily, talk, talk and talk again before you commit yourselves. A basis of trust and understanding is vital. That means understanding one's own attitude to money which is often conditioned by past experience. Try to look ahead calmly and without emotion."*

---

I've been told that financial planning can be as easy as ABC:

- **Accounts** – what income you have, where it has to go
- **Budgets** – how you will make your income work to match your expenditure
- **Checks** – regular checking to be sure the right amount of money is in the right place, at the right time, for the right reason

Planning for a stepfamily can be a little more complicated because of the additional factors to take into account and because of the amount of family change. But there have always been different kinds of families and families have always had to deal with change. Clearly, when families do change there are many questions to answer, plans to consider and decisions to make. At times of change all families need help. We hope this book will help you and your stepfamily through the changes that are facing you at the moment and in the years to come.

Erica De'Ath

*Founder Member and Chief Executive*
National Stepfamily Association

### References

Estess, PS (1992) *Remarriage and Your Money: Once again, for richer or poorer,* Little Brown.

*General Household Survey 1991* (1993) HMSO Publications.

Haskey, J (1994) Stepfamilies and stepchildren in Great Britain, *Population Trends,* No. 76, Summer, HMSO Publications.

### Note!

The information in this book is based on the law in England and Wales. If you live in Scotland or Northern Ireland you will find certain differences in law and common practices, and you should always check with a local lawyer or advice agency.

Wherever you live you should be aware that there are proposals to amend many of the laws and current practices which affect the family. Many of these changes have been mentioned in the book, but they may take years before they reach the statute books. You should always ask your legal adviser to explain the current position to you. In addition, regulations concerning eligibility for, and payment levels of, State benefits are under constant review and are likely to change from time to time.

# PART ONE

## TALKING ABOUT MONEY

Love it or loathe it, filthy lucre is a fact of life. Money may make the world go round but it can be a rough ride. For stepfamilies where the financial pot is likely to be more thinly and more intricately spread, the road can be especially tough.

Money matters are the biggest source of arguments in families. As family units become more complex and finances more sophisticated, the opportunities for hearthside tensions are likely to soar.

Stepfamilies face particularly difficult financial challenges. Not only are the calls on your resources likely to be bigger but in the aftermath of a separation or divorce your funds will probably be depleted. Add to this the emotional and practical financial baggage of a previous relationship and the demands of the new one and you have the recipe for a good deal of financial strife.

---

*"Children are the emotional touchstone so try and be honest with each other when you are annoyed over money matters and not take it out on the kids, especially if it is an ex-partner who is causing the trouble."*

---

Managing your money may not be easy, but it needn't become a trauma either. Part One: Talking About Money is here to help you identify and face up to your personal financial challenges so that handling your financial affairs becomes a more productive experience.

Many people find it almost impossible to talk about money. Whether out of boredom, ignorance or sheer embarrassment, finances leave lots of us lost for words. Money, like death and sex, remains a great taboo. Brought up in a world of hushed whisperings and 'don't tells', arguments and red faces, is it any wonder that so many adults grow up to be incapable of straight and confident financial dealing? Discussing finances within stepfamilies can be especially fraught. There may be a host of unspoken concerns and qualms and a sense of continually walking on financial eggshells.

On the following pages you will find a series of exercises and quizzes. They are not intended as an in-depth probe into your financial psyche but as a starting point for further thought and discussion.

Financial planning is not everyone's idea of a good time; it is, however, a necessity if you and your extended family want to stay both sane and solvent. You may never learn to love it, but you might as well let go of the angst.

## THINKING ABOUT MONEY

Are you a big spender or a money meanie? Do bank statements send you running for cover or do you relish the cut and thrust of balancing your books? Is your cash machine the victim of the latest teenage trainer demand? Just what kind of a money manager are you and who really pulls your purse strings?

Fearful or frustrated, comfortable or challenged, angry or excited, how you feel about money will dictate just how effectively you plan and negotiate your financial affairs.

Money can be a very emotional issue. Yet unlike other emotional issues like love and relationships we spend very little time thinking about why we react the way we do towards money. Many factors contribute to the way we feel about and handle our finances. Perhaps if we took time to explore what makes our internal counting systems tick, we'd be able to deal with our own financial business more successfully.

> *"We have a good financial relationship, we share what we both have. We discuss money matters and try to avoid hiccups."*

The following exercises are intended as much for entertainment as for self-revelation. There are no right or wrong answers. You might like to try them out with other members of your stepfamily: they may help break the financial ice. The Money Quiz is strictly for fun – although it may prove to be revealing!

## The money quiz

Are you a cheque stub champion or a cheque stub charlie? There is a theory that how you complete – or don't complete – your cheque book stubs is a fairly good indicator of how you handle your finances. Since cheque books are creeping out of fashion you'll have to take this measure of pecuniary responsibility with a fair dose of salt.

How would you answer the following questions? Tick the statement that most closely reflects your own response in each case.

*1. What do you think about cash – coins and paper notes?*
☐ A. Great stuff, it means you've got something to spend.

☐ B. I like the sensation of cash, it feels like real money.

☐ C. It's dangerous to carry too much cash about.

☐ D. Using a credit card is so much cleaner.

*2. Have you any idea where all your money is?*
☐ A. Who knows, but you can't get worked up over every last penny.

☐ B. I more or less know where I stand but I could find out in detail.

☐ C. I can put my finger on every last pound.

☐ D. There's £5 on the mantelpiece.

*3. What would you do if you found yourself in debt?*
☐ A. Not a lot. Everyone owes money, debt's a fact of life.

☐ B. Talk to my creditors immediately.

☐ C. I wouldn't get into debt, I'd rather go without.

☐ D. Run away.

*4. Are credit cards a good thing?*

☐ A. They're a great way of shopping when you haven't got the cash.

☐ B. They're useful providing you can pay the bill each month.

☐ C. Dangerous, because you get tempted to spend what you haven't got.

☐ D. At least it makes spending seem unreal.

*5. Do you think it's worth sorting out a pension?*

☐ A. I'd rather spend the money now than save up for an old age I might not live to see.

☐ B. Yes, even if it's only a bit.

☐ C. I'd put all my savings into my retirement.

☐ D. It's horrible even to think about a pension, I'll get by.

*6. What about savings?*

☐ A. They're okay in theory. In practice my money tends to get spent.

☐ B. I like to save what I can and I think it's worth taking some risks with your money.

☐ C. I prefer to keep my money in the building society where I can see it.

☐ D. Who do you think I am, a millionaire?

*7. Is professional financial advice important?*

☐ A. My mate's got a sharp nose for financial deals.

☐ B. Yes, providing you shop around and check out the information you get.

☐ C. I'd rather talk to someone I know well than rely on the advice of a 'professional' stranger.

☐ D. You wouldn't catch me anywhere near a bank manager or financial adviser.

*8. Do you fill in your cheque book stubs?*

☐ A. What's a cheque book stub?

☐ B. Usually who it's to and how much for.

☐ C. Yes, every line, every time.

☐ D. I haven't seen my cheque book for some time.

## How did you do?

**MOSTLY As** Easy come, easy go, that's you. So you get your fingers burnt but you reckon you'll live to see another day. Laid back is fine, but there's a danger that you'll end up comatose and penniless and your family won't thank you for either. Hang on to the low stress levels but gear up your financial acumen. Unless you mend your ways you'll remain a definite cheque stub charlie!

**MOSTLY Bs** You seem to have it about right. You're not a numismatic nutter but you take a keen interest in sorting out your financial affairs. Although you get to be a cheque stub champion, don't rest on your laurels. You'll find yourself running into problems unless you review your financial situation regularly.

**MOSTLY Cs** Do you tie yourself in knots about everything? Relax. Counting out your piggy bank is fine but perhaps you ought to ease up, be a little daring, risk a little more and you could reap some rich rewards. Cheque stub cautious you may be, unbend and you could end up a champion.

**MOSTLY Ds** You're a complete money phobic. The sight of a £10 note sends you into a cold sweat. There's nothing very grand about some basic financial planning. If you don't get a grip on your greenbacks you'll find yourself in a complete financial fuddle. Change your cheque stub charlie ways and get yourself on course to becoming a champion.

## The hot brass brainstorm

Test your money reflexes with this quick financial brainstorm (for more on brainstorming see page 42). Write down the words or phrases that immediately come into your head when you think about the following:

1. Money and finance.
2. Your current financial situation.

If you find it difficult to think spontaneously, you might like to choose the words that you associate with each of the above phrases from the following lists:

1. Fun • fear • status • boredom • distaste • fascination • control excitement • vulgar • nightmare • underhand • pleasure • arguments guilt • priority • interest • confident • embarrassment • know-how hatred • enjoyment • tedious • power • stress • challenge • sleepless nights • nausea • useful • anxiety

2.  Organised • overwhelmed • ignorant • under control • tense
    upfront • frightened • embarrassed • secretive • angry
    depressed • challenged • frustrated • soul destroying
    confident • worried • guilty • in limbo • isolated
    resentful • complicated • manageable • protective • optimistic

Have a look at your lists. Do you have in front of you a set of
dynamic and positive words? Or is your list downbeat? Which
negative descriptions would you like to change? Pick out one in
particular. Ask yourself what it would take to eliminate that word
from your list or turn it into something positive. Now, using the
other exercises and information in this book see if you can achieve
your goal.

## Investigating your financial baggage

Whatever situation we find ourselves in, whether we're
embarking on a new relationship or going on safari in the outback,
we travel with a good deal of emotional baggage. This baggage contains all the experiences we've ever accumulated, the good times and
the bad. The same can be applied to how we deal with our finances.
The way we are brought up to understand and take responsibility
for financial matters, the impact of an acrimonious divorce, the effect
of making a lot of cash or relying on benefits, all these shape how we
feel about handling money.

---

*"My husband's insistence on giving the same to each child
regardless of need in order to seem 'fair' used to be a big issue."*

---

Money is the thread that binds the diverse and often tenuous
links between extended stepfamily networks. Within the melee of
relationships, it's the M word – maintenance – that often looms
large. Money in one side and money out the other. That simple
transfer of cash can be loaded with emotion. Resentment at what's
seen as an uneven redistribution of resources or anger at a perceived
failure by one party to meet their obligations. Money is the ghost
of previous relationships that can come to haunt the new. You
may never be able to lay it to rest, but you can attempt to render its
presence relatively benign.

---

*"My desire to give to my children and grandchildren can be a
source of tension."*

---

As children grow older they become more keenly aware about the true currency of relative wealth and the transfer of money. They may feel confused by the different financial experiences they confront in each family unit. They may try to establish their ranking in the extended family order by demanding to know exactly who gets what in the maintenance stakes. In this way, money becomes the measure of status and power. It can also become a tool for manipulation.

---

*"We went through a phase when the only time my stepchildren came was when they wanted something."*

---

If your family financial negotiations always end in a bust up, or you bring down the mental shutters at the mention of money, it's worth exploring why this might be so. The aim of the next few exercises is to help you put into perspective your family's financial past in order to provide an insight into how you might deal positively with your financial future.

### Exercise One

Tick which of the following statements most closely reflects your own beliefs and experiences about:

**Growing up**

(You may wish to substitute someone more appropriate for 'parents')

☐ My parents were extremely cautious, they only spent what they had.

☐ There were constant arguments about money.

☐ I was conscious of being different from other children because of my family's financial situation.

☐ Money was a taboo subject.

☐ My parents were very free and easy with their money, even if they got into debt.

☐ Money dominated our lifestyle.

☐ I vowed that financially I'd be very different from my parents.

### The family and financial support
(Family in this context means parents, siblings and other blood relatives)

☐ My family think it's up to me to sort myself out financially.

☐ There's no question my family would give whatever they could.

☐ I'd never dream of asking family or friends for help.

☐ I think it's my duty to stick by my family financially.

☐ I can't take financial responsibility for other people's mistakes.

☐ My family expects too much of me financially.

### Your partner

☐ We pool all our resources and regard everything we own as belonging to us equally.

☐ As far as possible we each keep our financial affairs completely private.

☐ I leave all the financial dealings to my partner – I don't know what decisions have been taken.

☐ We talk everything through and usually agree on what to do.

☐ Every time we talk about money we end up rowing.

☐ We don't tend to discuss money, things just happen.

☐ My partner and I have very different attitudes towards money.

☐ I feel very protective towards 'my' money.

### The impact of previous relationship(s)

☐ My previous relationship has affected the way I now approach money matters.

☐ I resent the way my partner's past has made an impact on my/our family's financial situation.

☐ My financial relationship with my current partner is very different from the one I had with my previous partner(s).

☐ My current partner resents any financial contribution to our family from my former partner.

☐ I feel angry that my earnings are taken into account when assessing maintenance for my partner's children.

☐ My partner's ex doesn't keep up with maintenance payments and that makes me feel resentful towards my stepchildren.

**Your children**

☐ My children do/don't understand the financial pressures on me.

☐ I feel differently about my financial responsibilities towards my birth children and my stepchildren.

☐ The children from my different relationships make different financial demands on me.

☐ I find it easy to talk to my children about money issues.

☐ My birth children and stepchildren have different experiences of money and wealth which causes me concern.

☐ My birth/stepchildren are very manipulative about money.

☐ My birth children and my stepchildren have very different attitudes to money.

☐ I worry that I can't provide the same material benefits for my children as my former partner/other units in the extended step-family.

What kind of patterns have emerged? Are your financial lifestyle and your approach to money similar to those of your parents or radically different? What kind of impact have previous relationships had on your attitude towards money? Do you treat your own children in the way you were treated? What in your experience has made it particularly easy or especially difficult to talk about money? Is there any statement that you've ticked that you would like to try and change?

> ### · Exercise Two

Think in turn about the different attitudes you, your partner (or your ex-partner) and your own children and stepchildren have towards money. You might like to do this as a brainstorming exercise (see page 42) or you could select appropriate descriptions from the list below:

cautious • confident • spendthrift • ignorant • happy go lucky obsessive • anxious • informed • naive • non assertive • frightened hungry • unconcerned • worldly • unappreciative • negotiator muddled • mean • greedy

How similar or dissimilar are your views? Where there are differences, are they really very great? Why do you think your family hold the attitudes you see them as having?

NB It would be well worth checking out your analysis of your family's attitudes. You may find that they would each describe themselves very differently! If you can, sit down and talk about those differences – give examples of why you picked the descriptions you did. Are your views justified?

---

*"I think my eight year old stepson expects too much from us financially. He stays with us at weekends and comes on holidays and we provide for him. He also gets presents almost every weekend."*

---

### Exercise Three

This exercise will help you identify how comfortable you feel in dealing with different people in various financial situations. It has the potential to become a very long exercise indeed – so you might want to tackle it a bit at a time!

Here are five money moments:

- Asking for money
- Refusing a request for money
- Asking for some financial information
- Making a financial plan
- Negotiating a financial agreement

Now think how you would feel if you were in each of the above situations with each of the people listed below. Give yourself a rating of 1 to 5 for each money moment according to how comfortable or uncomfortable you would feel. (Not all money moments will apply in each case, so use what's appropriate.)

The 'scoring' ranges from 1 = I would find this situation extremely uncomfortable/impossible to deal with to 5 = I would find this situation extremely comfortable and easy to deal with.

- ☐ Current partner
- ☐ Former partner(s)
- ☐ Birth children
- ☐ Stepchildren
- ☐ Parent or guardian
- ☐ Sibling
- ☐ Close friend

- [ ] Employer or clients
- [ ] Government agency,
  e.g. Benefits Agency or Child Support Agency
- [ ] Solicitor
- [ ] Bank or building society manager
- [ ] Financial adviser

Hopefully your responses will enable you to distinguish a pattern of successful and less successful financial dealings. Look carefully at your lowest score marks. Are they mostly against one person or against one money moment? Is it the situation or the person who makes you feel most uncomfortable?

---

*"I am conscious that we shouldn't treat our daughter and my stepson differently. But I'm worried that we won't be able to maintain equality if we continue to give our stepson presents so often."*

---

## CASH COMMUNICATION

Money is an extremely emotive subject. As the last chapter will have highlighted, few people feel comfortable dealing with every financial situation. You may be confident negotiating with your bank manager or some other independent person but find it difficult to talk openly about money with those closest to you, especially if you believe your ex-spouse or your partner's ex is causing you hardship. The following pages suggest some practical ways to help you manage more effectively in all financial situations, no matter how difficult they might be.

**Watch out!** Just because you always appear to get your own way whenever you talk about money, it does not automatically mean that you deal with such situations effectively. So if you think this might apply to you, keep reading!

WATCH OUT!

### The feel good factor

Think back to the last discussion you had about money. It may have been with your former spouse regarding maintenance or your current partner about a holiday – or it could have been a pocket money dispute with your stepchildren or a general talk with a financial adviser or bank manager. What was the outcome of your talk?

Did you leave feeling good or irritated? Or was the whole thing frustratingly inconclusive? Which of the following six statements bests sums up what happened:

- [ ] I went along with what was decided but I didn't really agree. I'm sure I'll find a way out of it.
- [ ] It was a real slanging match and we went right off the subject.
- [ ] I got what I wanted but the other person looked dissatisfied.
- [ ] I felt the other person didn't listen to what I said. I wasn't happy with the outcome.
- [ ] I think the other person had already made a decision, it was a waste of time having a discussion.
- [ ] Both/all of us said how we felt and we reached an agreement/compromise.

If you've ticked anything other than the last statement, then you could be heading for trouble. So-called agreements which leave one person steaming, frustrated, angry or humiliated rarely work out. When it comes to talking about money the feel good factor really matters. That doesn't mean that everyone sits around on cloud nine. It does mean that you're able to express what you think and feel openly and that you enable others to do the same.

Whether you find yourself dominating the discussion, inventing ways to circumvent the outcome or utterly unable to articulate what you're thinking, here are six tips on each of the three most important communication skills: speaking your mind; listening to enable; criticising constructively.

## Speaking your mind

This isn't about a dose of aggressive verbal diarrhoea. It is about being able to channel your thoughts and express coherently and accurately what's going on in your head. Here are the first set of cash communication tips:

1. Engage your brain before you open your mouth. Run through what you're going to say. Then run through it again. Consider how the other person could react and work out what your response might be.

2. Use the word 'I' when you speak. Don't palm your views off on to some imaginary friend. Avoid using phrases like 'People think ...' or 'It's...' Learn to say 'I feel...', 'I think...'

3. Express your feelings. Keep away from 'Can't you guess what's wrong with me?' games of sulking and stomping. It's much better to say how you feel. Try saying 'I feel angry/happy/comfortable/appreciated/let down/irritated when...'

4. If you want to state an opinion or make a demand:
   - decide what you want to say,
   - say it,
   - stick to it and say it over again if you have to.

5. If someone wants to turn your discussion into an argument, don't take the bait or you may end up fuelling World War Three. Acknowledge what the other person says and then repeat your statement or demand. For example:

   MICHAEL: *I'm really sorry but I forgot to bank your maintenance cheque today.*

   KELLY: *You idiot. Only you could be that stupid and unreliable – how are we going to buy the kids' school uniforms this weekend? Can't you get anything right?*

   MICHAEL: *Look, I'm sorry. I agree it was a stupid thing to do. There's nothing I can do now. I'll bank it on Monday and I'll knock off early on Thursday so we can go late night shopping.*

6. Think about how you say things as much as what you say. Look people in the eye. Smile if you're happy, don't smile if you're not. Control both table thumping and nervous twitching.

## Listening to enable

Own up! How many times have you been in conversation with someone and found yourself yelling at them in exasperation, 'But you're not listening to me!'? Talking to somebody who continually stares into space or butts into your sentences can be an incredibly frustrating and lonely experience. Few people are natural listeners but the skills can be learnt. Here are the second set of cash communication tips.

1. Listen with your whole body, not just your ears. Look at the person who's talking to you. Don't stare them out but make regular eye contact. Lean forward, keen to hear what they have to say.

2. Cut out other distractions such as a TV or radio or screaming kids. If someone has something important to say, give them undivided space and attention.

3. Help people to open up. Don't tell them to 'Cheer up' or 'Snap out of it'. Throw them an opening lifeline by, for example,' describing their behaviour, 'You look a bit down today' or 'You look on top of the world'. Invite them to talk to you, 'Do you want to talk about it?' or 'Go on…'

4. Don't interrupt. The odd 'hmm', 'yes' or 'really' is sufficient to show you're listening and prompt them to continue.

5. Respond positively. This doesn't mean take the floor and deliver a speech on your theory of the world. Try and sum up what the person has said, 'You feel you're in a dilemma...', 'There's so much going on you don't know what to do next...'

6. Know when to stop and re-focus the discussion. If you're in a sticky situation and you're pouring your heart out it can be difficult to see the wood for the trees. If you find the conversation going round and round in circles, help the talker to focus on their priorities or their next action. Remember, it's much better to let the other person come to their own conclusion than to attempt to map out your own solutions for them.

## Criticising constructively

After a childhood of playground taunts about being 'spotty' or 'stupid', 'brainy' or an 'airhead', is it any wonder that adults emerge unable to give or take criticism? Every day we involve ourselves in small and great acts of criticism from complaints about shoddy work to a compliment about a new hairstyle. Criticism can be good or bad, but it should never be destructive. Here are the third set of cash communication tips.

1. Don't beat about the bush, get straight to the point. Forget about the 'I hope you don't mind me saying this but...' and try instead, 'I want to talk to you about...'

2. Avoid labelling the person and instead describe their behaviour. Don't say, 'You're a stupid, irresponsible spendthrift.' Do say, 'I thought it was irresponsible of you to spend our last £10 on a bottle of champagne.'

3. Be specific about what's wrong and be specific about what you want done. 'I feel really frustrated when you don't include me in your discussions with the bank manager. Next time you go, I want to come along too.'

4. Don't automatically defend yourself or accept criticism. Ask yourself whether all or some of it is justified. If it is, acknowledge it gracefully, 'Yes, you're right about that, I didn't give it enough thought. I'm sorry, I'll see what I can do about it.'

5. If the criticism isn't valid, say so. 'Yes, perhaps I've been forgetful before, but I don't think that's justified on this occasion...'

6. Give sincere compliments often. When someone says something complimentary to you, respond positively and not with a brush off.

Finally here are three practical ways that you can help yourself deal with particularly difficult situations.

## Difficult dealings

1. If you feel angry and het up learn to keep your emotions in check before you utter a word. Ask yourself, 'Just how important is this issue and exactly what am I feeling?' Then begin what you have to say by acknowledging your feelings, I feel dissatisfied / impatient / cross / infuriated / absolutely incensed... (As you see there are lots of degrees of anger – make sure you don't blow all your fuses before you begin!)

2. Write yourself a little gameplan in advance. Imagine the meeting place. In reality, if you have the choice, go somewhere where you won't be interrupted. Write down what you want to say. Try and judge the other person's mood and their responses.

3. Go for practical solutions. It's much better to say, 'I know this situation's difficult but let's work together to find a way out. How about...' than go round in circles re-inventing past wheels.

## HOW TO NEGOTIATE THE BOTTOM LINE

Negotiation is not the prerogative of summit bound world leaders. From the supermarket checkout queue to the kids' bathtime, pay rises at work to the Chinese take-away, we're all at it – negotiating our own little deals. The important things are to make the negotiation process productive and to make the agreement stick.

There are six golden rules to negotiating effectively:

1. Don't attempt to score points. Negotiation is not a battle – there are no victors and no vanquished. If you think you've 'won', it'll be a phoney victory.

2. Aim to reach a fair compromise. This means it's likely that no one will get exactly what they were after, but on balance everyone will be satisfied.

3. Be realistic. Keep your demands well moderated. Outline your priorities and your concerns. Be prepared to listen.

4. Seek the views of everyone affected by the outcome of the negotiations. Acknowledge and respond constructively to their concerns and views.

5. Never be so passive that you give up everything you want or believe in – you'll only feel resentful later on.

6. Ensure that whatever you agree on will actually work when put into practice. If you compromise on something that's pie in the sky, your negotiations will have been in vain.

## Negotiation: the process

Negotiation is about getting to a chorus of 'yes'! Essentially you start out with a broadly common goal, for example agreeing how much you'll spend on a holiday. Then, like a table tennis game, the proposals, counter proposals and technicalities are served back and forth. Eventually the 'game' concludes when all the issues have been aired and an agreement or compromise reached.

The critical thing is to ensure that all the players leave the arena with their self-esteem and their integrity still intact. In the event of stalemate, the players can call in an independent umpire – in the case of family legal and financial disputes, the court – to settle their differences.

Here are the seven stages of the negotiation process:

### Stage One: Setting a common goal

Unless you set out the aim of the negotiations you may find each person proceeding along parallel lines with little hope of ever making contact. This will make your discussions frustrating and ultimately fruitless. You may have to do some work in order to identify your common goal. Sometimes a sense of anger, fear or hopelessness can get in the way of working out what the issue really is.

*Joely and Simon are concerned about Simon's 23-year-old son, James, who's arrived in their home town looking for work. He's staying in a squat with some friends and from his recent visits to them it seems that without a phone or a permanent address he's finding job hunting hard. They both agree that James needs some practical help.*

### Stage Two: Establishing individual objectives

You need to be clear about what each you of you expects, and wants to achieve, out of the negotiation process. You also need to think about your 'bottom line', the point beyond which matters become non-negotiable.

*Simon wants to help his son financially, he'd also like to offer James a home with his second family. After Simon's divorce, James went to live with his mother and Simon had very little contact with his son. He feels this is an opportunity to make up for the past. Although Joely is concerned about James's welfare, money is tight and she's worried that James would become an additional financial burden. She thinks that James's mother spoilt him and it's up to him to fend for himself now. Joely believes she already has a full house with her own two teenage children and her and Simon's toddler. She's very reluctant to invite James to stay.*

## Stage Three: Voicing priorities and concerns

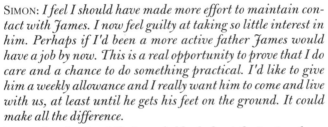

Having established your individual objectives, it's now important to communicate your feelings and thoughts to the other person. This is where the skills of speaking your mind and listening begin to play an important part (see pages 36–38).

Simon and Joely's conversation might go something like this:

SIMON: *I feel I should have made more effort to maintain contact with James. I now feel guilty at taking so little interest in him. Perhaps if I'd been a more active father James would have a job by now. This is a real opportunity to prove that I do care and a chance to do something practical. I'd like to give him a weekly allowance and I really want him to come and live with us, at least until he gets his feet on the ground. It could make all the difference.*

JOELY: *I understand that you feel bad about the past and you think this is an opportunity to put things right between you. However, we've already got a full house and things are tight financially. There simply isn't room for him here and I don't think we've got the spare cash to help. James has been used to getting his own way and I think he might just take advantage of all of us.*

SIMON: *I can see you're concerned about how he might affect our family. I don't think it'll make a big difference to our budget and besides I think he's grown up a lot. I feel hurt that you seem so resistant to the idea of him coming to live here.*

JOELY: *The important thing for me is to ensure that our family life doesn't suffer, our priority has got to be the younger children. I wouldn't mind him staying as a stop gap but I'm worried he might just think it's a soft option and never get round to leaving.*

## Stage Four: Brainstorm your options and find out the facts

The point about brainstorming ideas is that you just pour out everything that comes into your head, no matter how daft or impossible it might appear. When no one can come up with any more schemes, then you go back and weed out the really crazy and unworkable ones.

Once you've whittled down your ideas to a few real choices you need to think just how effectively they can be put into practice, whether there will be any technical hiccups, how these might be overcome and so on. Your aim is to ensure that when you return to the last stages of the negotiation process you know that in front of you are practical, workable options.

*Since neither Joely nor Simon knows what James's reaction might be to the idea of staying with them, they agree to think through a list of possible options and their consequences. These are the three ideas that make their final list:*

*Simon could help out James financially so that he could find a flatshare of his own. Simon checks out local rents and finds that he can't afford to do this. Joely feels that Simon has paid out enough in maintenance and now, on a restricted income, his first duty ought to be to her and their children. Simon reluctantly agrees with this.*

*James could stay with them for a set period. He wouldn't be asked to make a contribution up front but he would be expected to help around the house and repay his phone bills. Since Joely refuses to have James sleeping in the living room, she will have to ask her teenage son to share his room. (She realises she may have to offer her own son some incentive to do this.)*

*James could use their house as a base, providing him with a stable address, a telephone and the odd meal and bath.*

## Stage Five: Check out your options

It may be that you've already been able to involve everyone affected by the outcome of the negotiation process. If you haven't had the chance to check out their views, then now's the time to do it. You've got your options in front of you but it's important to remain flexible. You may need to refine your ideas when you've heard what others have to say.

*Joely and Simon need to talk things through with three people, Joely's two children and James. They decide not to broach the financial issue as it's already clear that they can't offer James anything substantial.*

*Joely's daughter is nonplussed by the whole episode and has no feelings one way or another about James staying. Her son is less impressed, particularly at the notion of having to share his room. When they met on previous occasions, the two boys didn't really hit it off. Joely's son says he'll only tolerate James for a week.*

*When Simon talks to James, his son seems resentful at his interference although he understands he means well. James would prefer to take a raincheck on the offer to stay, but would welcome the chance to use the house as a base. James raises the issue of money and asks his father for some extra cash to see him through each week.*

## Stage Six: Decision time

This is the point at which you stop 'umming' and 'erring' and decide what course of action you're going to take. The two things you've got to ensure are that first, everyone is on board – though not necessarily enthusiastic – and second, that the decision you're about to take will actually work. At this stage you also need to agree any essential rules that you think will help make the decision stick.

*Joely and Simon invite James round for a meal together with Joely's children and their toddler. Round the table they agree that James can use the house as a base and that they'll give him a key. However, they also lay down some house rules. James is welcome to come round whenever he likes, but if he wants a meal then he has to let Joely know in advance. They also ask him not to turn their offer into open house for all his mates. They also say that if his phone bills become excessive, then they'll ask for a contribution.*

*When Simon has a chance to be alone with James he says that he cannot afford to give him a weekly allowance. However, he'll do whatever he can to help James in his search for a job. If he needs contacts, photocopying or fares then he'll see what he can do. Simon also asks James not to take their hospitality for granted and to make an effort to be sociable with Joely and the children. James agrees, albeit somewhat reluctantly, to the arrangements.*

You've now got to put into practice what you've agreed. If appropriate, you also need to decide on a date to review how the outcome of your negotiations is working. People will often agree to something new if they think that it's not cast in stone and can be changed if things don't work out. You should never enter an agreement on the basis that it isn't going to stick, but neither should you be so inflexible as to suggest that what you've decided can't be revised.

# COPING WITH CASH CONFLICTS

The biggest dilemma for most stepfamilies is the constant balancing of financial responsibilities: the need to satisfy competing demands from different members of current and former families. Inevitably when the money pot is limited you will have to make hard choices – not everyone can come first nor have their needs met in full.

---

*"I gladly support the children from both my marriages. I find it easy to talk to my children about money but not my stepchildren. My stepchildren have a lot of money in their own right through various trusts. They have all the latest gadgets and computers and my own children accept this."*

---

There is no easy solution or quick formula. In fact, the only financial formula for stepfamilies that you'll find in this entire book is related to the rigid calculations of the Child Support Act (see page 84). To some extent the courts and your personal financial situation will dictate what you do, but to a large degree you're on your own when it comes to making moral and emotional judgements about your responsibilities. The burden falls most often on the shoulders of men as stepfathers and non-resident parents. However, the repercussions are felt throughout the various family units.

Conflict over money, or the sharing out of available financial resources, is invariably an emotive issue. The first exercise which follows gives you the opportunity to articulate your grievances about particular demands made on you or your new partner. The second, is a practical exercise intended to help you get into perspective the relative rankings of the various financial responsibilities faced by you and your stepfamily. See also the section on Cash Communication, in particular 'Speaking your mind' (page 36).

> *"I was often made to feel guilty by my stepchildren because we have more than them – a nicer home, car and so on."*

## The money moan meter

Like many people in stepfamilies you may feel that you are at the constant financial beck and call of someone else – perhaps your or your partner's ex and their new family. Stepfamilies rarely break away completely from the threads that bind them, not only to their previous families but also to those of their new partner. You may have the sense that someone outside your immediate family unit has a stranglehold over your financial situation and therefore over much of the way you live and the choices you can make.

This is really a pillow-bashing, floor-stomping exercise giving you the chance to spit out who or what makes you enormously angry and frustrated. It's important to recognise that however annoyed or anguished you feel there may be absolutely nothing you can do about the situation. What matters is that you can say how you feel (see page 41). You may, however, be able to redress the balance by prioritising your or your partner's financial responsibilities – see later.

The money moan meter has three zones:

• <u>measly moans</u> – a pale yellow zone: things that make you jealous or envious.

• <u>medium moans</u> – an amber zone: things that are serious irritations or inconveniences but which don't fundamentally alter your lifestyle.

• <u>mega moans</u> – the red hot zone: things that really make a difference to your family life and your day-to-day existence.

Focus on the person whose financial dependence or interference you resent most. Now think of concrete complaints you have about that person's money demands.

*For example. Susanna focuses on her partner Jake's former wife, Kate, and Jake and Kate's two children. Her list begins:*

*1. CSA-assessed maintenance that Jake pays to Kate means we can't go on a decent holiday this year.*

*2. Jake gives more expensive birthday presents to his children than to ours just to save face with Kate.*

*3. Kate is demanding that Jake forks out to continue their kids' private education. Our children have to make do with the school round the corner.*

Now 'feed' each zone of the meter with one or more of your complaints, according to how important you feel each one is.

*For example, into the pale yellow 'measly moan' zone Susanna puts number 2. Essentially she feels jealous that Jake's children already have so many more toys and games than theirs. Into the amber 'medium moan' zone Susanna puts number 1 – she feels very put out that the family will miss out on a proper summer holiday this year. Into the red hot 'mega moan' zone Susanna puts number 3. She is eaten up with fury that Jake's children will reap the benefits of private education while their children won't even have the choice.*

You may find that simply articulating your anger to yourself, your partner or a friend may help ease the rage. It may also be helpful to divide up your frustration into manageable 'zones' as on the imaginary meter, and identify the really pressing concerns as against those which are basically irritants.

## The pecuniary push-me, pull-you

The aim of this exercise is to help you begin to prioritise your responsibilities to all the members of your family. You may find this useful to do when, for example, you are trying to write a will or reassess maintenance contributions. Obviously if you are using this exercise to establish maintenance priorities you will be constrained by the orders of the court or the Child Support Agency. Like many of the exercises there is no definitive answer, it simply provides a framework within which to evaluate your circumstances and establish possible solutions. You may find it useful to complete this exercise after having read some of the practical advice given in the early chapters of **Part Three: The Financial Essentials.**

You'll need one or more large pieces of paper, A4 or bigger, turned on the long side. Divide the sheet(s) into six vertical columns and number each one, left to right.

### Column 1: People

A   For whose financial welfare are you currently responsible?

List everyone who depends on you for money in some way – however minor. Your list might include: current and former spouses or partners; children; stepchildren; parents; parents-in-law; siblings. Leave plenty of space between names.

B   Is there anyone who is not currently on your list but for whom you feel some financial responsibility?

C   Is there anyone who is not on your current list who might reasonably be expected to make a financial demand on you in the next five or ten years?

For example, you and your partner might be considering having a baby.

## Column 2: Needs

What financial needs do you/ought you to meet for each of these people?

Itemise the main financial needs you meet for each person. You might include things like: total financial needs; housing; school fees; specific bills; nursing home; entertainment; childcare costs.

## Column 3: Responsibility

On a scale of 1–4, how 'morally' responsible do you feel about meeting each of these financial needs? (1= very responsible, 4 = not at all responsible.)

## Column 4: Challenge

Look at those names and situations which you marked with a 1 or 2. Ask yourself two questions.

A   What would happen if I withdrew or reduced my support?

B   How would that person manage?

Now look at those names and situations which you marked with a 3 or 4. Ask yourself two more questions.

C   If I don't feel particularly responsible for making this financial commitment, why am I doing it?

D    Has the recipient the right to expect me to make that financial commitment?

## Column 5: Changing needs

The aim of column 5 is to help you set out the monetary needs over the next 15 years of those for whom you take financial responsibility. (You can do this for a longer or shorter period if you like.) Take three different coloured pens – let's say you have to hand red, blue and green. The red represents the next 5 years; the blue represents years 5 to 10; green represents years 10 to 15.

Taking the red pen first, make a mark next to each name to indicate how that person's financial demands on you will change over the next five years. Use an up arrow for increase, a down arrow for decrease, and a circle to indicate they will stay the same. Repeat for each colour and timescale.

*For example, Bill is doing this exercise. One of the people he has identified in column 1 is his 13-year-old daughter Trisha. At the moment his main expenses for Trisha are her school fees. For the next five years he doesn't envisage much will change, so he marks a red circle by her name. In five years' time Trisha will be 18 and Bill hopes she will go to college, so although he'll still have a financial commitment it will be less than it is currently. He therefore marks a down arrow in blue. Finally he marks another down arrow in green since he hopes that by the age of 23 Trisha will no longer be making major financial demands on him.*

### Column 6: Prioritising

In the final column you can begin to prioritise the financial demands made on you.

You will have to look at all your columns to see the general trend of your obligations – the short-term, pressing needs, the longer term demands that will decline with time. You may decide that certain people no longer need your help or support in such quantities as you previously gave. Fresh priorities may have taken the place of previous but continuing financial commitments.

Again using your coloured marker system, list in order of priority each financial obligation in a five-year period: 1 is your most urgent priority, 2 your next most urgent and so on. The point about prioritising your commitments – whatever they are, time, money and so on – is that one thing always takes precedence over another. It's a question of 'on balance'.

While prioritising won't conjure up any more cash, it will help you to decide how to divide up what you've got. It may have also highlighted times in the foreseeable future when the financial demands made on you will be even greater. Whatever conclusion you've finally reached, you need to start from the realisation that you will probably not be able to meet every demand or every demand in full. You will also have to manage the disappointment and frustration of those whose demands you cannot meet. In addition, you will have to manage your own feelings of possible guilt at not being able, or willing, to meet those demands. Equally, you might feel relief at relinquishing a financial obligation.

**Watch out!** Check that your're not trying to prioritise an outgoing which is actually someone else's reponsibility. For example, perhaps an absent parent is not meeting their obligation to a stepchild. You may need to suggest to your partner that certain maintenance payments are revised.

WATCH OUT!

Before getting on to the legal and financial nuts and bolts, there is one last practical exercise that's worth taking the time to do.

## Writing a lifestyle agreement

In a new relationship – or even in an ageing one – it can be very difficult to sit down and talk about issues like money. After all, it's not the most romantic of subjects to discuss, let alone commit to paper. Unfortunately romance rarely keeps a relationship alive: day-to-day practicalities like paying the gas bill tend to overshadow the confetti and candlelight.

Later on in the book we look at cohabitation contracts and the limitations on the kind of things you can actually write into such a contract (see page 52). However, there's nothing to stop any couple, living together or married, from confronting some of the important aspects of coupledom in an informal lifestyle agreement. Such a document allows you to sit down and talk about some fairly critical things which otherwise, in the passion of the moment, may be swept under the carpet and left to fester. Remember that crucial issues such as your home, your money and what happens after your death should be dealt with in properly drawn up legal documents for which you should seek the advice of a solicitor.

You can include statements about any aspect of your life together. It's wise to start off with a few words about why you have written the agreement and how long it's supposed to last. Setting a time limit to review what you have written is always worthwhile, and it's important to be flexible and recognise that as your relationship progresses you may wish to change what you have written.

---

*"We discuss all our money matters but my husband handles all the finances."*

---

Here are some of the money issues you might like to address:

- How you will run your financial affairs – whether you will have one account or two.

- Your attitudes to savings.
- What you will do if you get into debt.
- Your plans for retirement, what you will each live on.
- Your working lives – what happens if one person is transferred or loses their job.
- Your home – where you will live, who will be responsible for day-to-day budgeting and paying the bills.
- Schooling – whether you intend to pay for private education and how you will do this.
- Maintenance – whether you need to review your arrangements. If you're not relying on benefits, how each partner feels about maintenance paid by a former partner.
- Your financial priorities towards independent children and stepchildren.
- Other financial responsibilities towards other family members.
- Financial help from the extended family.

## Moving on

So what have you learnt about your financial self? Are you essentially a confident money manager with a few rough edges to smooth out? Or is your entire existence tied up with overwhelming financial decisions? Does your anxiety about doing the right thing and making ends meet pervade everything else you undertake? Are you an eternal optimist or has a previously disastrous financial relationship scarred your money emotions?

**Part One: Talking About Money** has aimed to help you begin to fit together the emotional aspects of your financial life. Most of the exercises were intended simply as a pause for thought, a starting point for further discussion and perhaps deeper probing.

There's no doubt that when it comes to financial or legal affairs, knowledge is power. However, it's not enough simply to know what questions to ask or where to go for information. You need to be able to think logically and manage the sense of frustration that inevitably occurs when circumstances make it hard for you to achieve your goals. This is never truer than when it comes to dealing with money.

Acknowledging your strengths and weaknesses over finance-related matters and being able to communicate your demands and concerns effectively will help you make far more use of the information that follows in the rest of the book. Becoming aware of where your personal pecuniary pot-holes might lie is the first step in learning to manage your own and your family's finances more effectively.

# PART TWO

## CHANGING FAMILY FORTUNES

Separating from one partner to set up home with another, creating a part-time stepfamily or choosing to cohabit rather than marry will all have an impact on your financial situation. For many stepfamilies their extended network of family units is constantly changing its identity. A former spouse may marry a new partner and become a step-parent, a remarriage may break down leaving an ex-partner more dependent on child maintenance, step-parents may have a baby of their own. This section looks at the legal entangling and disentangling of different kinds of relationships. It also explains the rights and responsibilities of parents, whether married or unmarried, birth, step or adoptive. It is important to understand the legal obligations and requirements that these 'life stage' events involve in order to appreciate some of the financial consequences. In particular, in this section you will find information about spousal and child maintenance.

## MAKING RELATIONSHIPS
### Cohabitation

The plain fact is that the law doesn't recognise cohabitation as a legally valid partnership between a man and a woman. Although the law imposes certain obligations on married couples, it makes no similar demands on people who cohabit. By the same token, while married couples can ultimately turn to the courts for justice if the relationship turns sour, the law offers cohabitees very little similar protection.

#### Cohabitation myths

There are many myths about the 'rights' of couples who live together 'as man and wife' but choose not to get married. Here are the most popular ones laid to rest.

- The term 'common law wife' or 'common law husband' has no legal significance. Common law marriages were abolished in the mid-eighteenth century, although Scotland retains something called 'marriage by cohabitation with habit and repute'.
- Although you may live together as husband and wife, unless you are actually married you have no automatic rights to your family home or to maintenance if you split up.

- The length of your relationship doesn't make any difference, you don't acquire any additional 'rights' as time goes on. Your legal position remains the same whether you cohabit for two weeks or 25 years.
- Cohabitees do not automatically inherit their partner's estate when one of them dies. Only by making a will can you guarantee that your surviving partner will be provided for.

Since the legal system will not automatically pick up the pieces when cohabiting relationships go wrong, it is absolutely critical to plan ahead and protect yourself. Remember, even if your relationship lasts a lifetime, death does not distinguish between married and unmarried couples. The law, however, does.

*"The experience of our previous relationships gave us greater awareness of the need to talk things through thoroughly and to get down to formal agreements on property."*

### Cohabitation contracts

A cohabitation contract is a private agreement made by a couple stating that they intend to live together and setting out the terms of their relationship. Cohabitation contracts can cover everything from where you live and how you deal with money to your attitudes towards child rearing and your social life. However, it's doubtful to what extent an English court of law would ever uphold or enforce some, or all, of the terms of such a contract.

English law can be incredibly contradictory. On the one hand, it upholds the right of individuals to make contracts between themselves. This would suggest that there is a place for cohabitation contracts. On the other hand, family law argues that it would not be in the interests of public policy for the courts to enforce agreements about some kinds of very private matters.

With this in mind, it's best to play safe and distinguish between those matters such as property and money that will stand up in court and the lifestyle issues that probably won't.

If you want to set down what will happen to your home and your finances if you split up, get a solicitor to draw up your wishes in the form of a trust deed. You'd be advised to get professional advice because these kind of documents need to conform to certain procedures if they are going to carry any weight. Remember, clauses that deal with the welfare of children can never be binding.

At the same time there's nothing to stop you writing an informal and separate 'lifestyle agreement' (see page 49). This can provide a framework within which to talk about and evaluate some important aspects of your relationship like sharing possessions, involving former partners, having children and spending money.

### Protecting yourself

For peace of mind cohabitees need to think about three key things:

1. <u>A roof over your head</u>. Unless you legally own the home you share with your partner you have no automatic right either to live there or to claim a financial interest in the property.

2. <u>Your money</u>. As far as cohabitees go, the law is not necessarily concerned with a fair redistribution of wealth. What's clearly yours will remain yours, what's been put into the communal pot will be divided in two. If you decide to dispense with individual bank and savings accounts and put all your cash into one coffer, watch out. If you split up, you may not get your money out in the same proportion as you put it in.

3. <u>Your will</u>. If you or your partner dies without making a will, then your property will be divided up according to the intestacy rules (see page 125). These only recognise blood relatives and make no provision for cohabitees. What's more, at the moment opportunities for cohabitees to challenge a will are very limited and court action can be difficult and time consuming (see page 126).

Out of necessity, cohabitees need to be self-sufficient. That applies not just to your home, your money and what happens when you or your partner dies, but to other areas of financial planning such as pension provision and life assurance. These are explained in greater detail in **Part Three: The Financial Essentials.**

## Engagement

Since getting engaged has no legal effect, the law attaches little significance to it. There are no legal formalities or requirements and you can become engaged before you're 16 without needing anyone's consent.

An engagement is no longer regarded as a legally binding contract. So if you call the whole thing off neither party can sue the other for any costs they've incurred in planning the wedding. If you do break up then you should return any presents you've been given, including those exchanged between prospective bride and groom. There is just one exception – the engagement ring. This is presumed to be an absolute gift and is therefore non-returnable.

If, after buying a home together you split up and can't decide how to divide up your property, then ultimately you can go to court. However, this will be expensive and you'd be better off sorting things out between you.

## Marriage

The traditional nuptial promise of mutual support and respect is not simply a romantic or spiritual sentiment. The act of marriage imposes on you three basic legal obligations. These are:

- the duty to cohabit, in other words to live together,
- the duty to maintain each other,
- the duty to have sex.

However, in reality a court of law would never force you to carry out any of these obligations, with one exception – the duty to maintain each other. As explained in other chapters, this requirement may continue to apply even when the relationship ends through separation, divorce or bereavement.

### Pre-nuptial contracts

Unfortunately these are a celluloid fantasy confined to American legal soaps. Pre-nuptial contracts, like cohabitation contracts, may be recognised in other parts of the world but they have no legal standing in the UK and cannot be legally binding.

The reason is that 'the powers that be' consider it contrary to public interest to allow couples to enter into a marriage having already drawn up a document detailing what would happen in the event of the relationship breaking down. They feel that such a contract would undermine the notion of 'until death us do part' and would create a presumption that marriage may not be a life-long commitment.

However, more and more engaged couples are drawing up a form of pre-nuptial contract stating how they would want to divide up their assets in the event of the marriage breaking down. While a court is unlikely to be obliged to adhere to these wishes, a judge may well take them in to consideration in determining how the assets should be split. Married couples may also want to write their own lifestyle agreement (see page 49).

## Who can marry?

To be legally valid, a marriage must fulfil six qualifications.

1. Both partners must agree voluntarily to marry and be capable of understanding the meaning of their consent.

2. Both partners must be single, widowed or divorced. If you've been separated from your spouse for many years and you've lost contact, then you should ask the court to grant you a divorce based on five years' separation (see page 68). This will avoid the risk of a bigamy prosecution.

3. Both partners must be over the age of 16. Young people under the age of 18 will need the signed consent of their parents and/or those with parental responsibility. In the case of divorced parents, this may mean the parent who has the residence order.

4. Both partners need to be mentally capable of understanding their actions at the time of the wedding ceremony itself. In addition they need to be physically capable, in other words able to consummate the marriage. However, if you marry someone in the full knowledge that they cannot consummate the marriage, then you cannot later have the marriage annulled (see page 67).

5. Partners must be of the opposite sex. Homosexual and lesbian marriages are not legally valid, nor are those where one partner • has undergone a sex change.

6. Partners must not be closely related. The law prohibits marriages between certain members of the family, for example between a stepfather and his stepdaughter or an aunt and her nephew. These are known as the prohibited degrees.

In addition to fulfilling these six qualifying terms you will have to follow the proper procedural formalities of the marriage itself.

## Wedding formalities

In England and Wales there are three ways you can get married legally:

- A civil, non-religious ceremony performed in accordance with statutory requirements.

- A wedding performed according to the rites of the Church of England.

- A religious ceremony by certain recognised denominations and faiths which meets essential regulations laid down by the state.

In order to proceed with a wedding ceremony you will need to complete a number of formalities and obtain the right kind of licence, for which there will be a fee. In practice, if you have a church or other religious wedding, your Minister should help you through this process.

Until recently you could only have a wedding service in a church or register office. New rules mean that other venues such as hotels can now apply for a licence to hold a wedding ceremony. For historic reasons, Jews and Quakers can hold marriage services where they like. However, these ceremonies must also adhere to certain legal requirements.

### Remarriage

You can only remarry if:

- your former partner is dead, .
- your previous marriage has been annulled,
- you have been granted a divorce decree absolute.

When you remarry, you will again take on the rights and responsibilities of a married person.

If you are about to remarry but haven't yet applied for or finalised the financial element of your divorce, you need to think about the following:

- You must check that any financial claims you intend to make against your former spouse are made before you remarry. Once you go through with your next marriage you won't be able to start a claim for a lump sum or property adjustment order (see page 76). However, if you have already begun a claim you can continue with it after the new marriage.
- If you have already remarried or you have a clear intention to do so, then the court will take this into consideration when making its judgment. If you deliberately deceive the court about your future intentions in order to succeed in making a claim, your former spouse may apply to have the decision overturned.

Although lump sum and property adjustment orders will not be affected by remarriage, periodical maintenance payments will cease. If you continue to receive payments, then your former spouse will be entitled to go to court to recover the money which he or she has paid out unnecessarily.

If, for whatever reason, you continue to make maintenance payments to a spouse who has remarried, you will not receive tax relief on them. If you are making payments to a former spouse, then these will not be affected by your own remarriage. However, if you have taken on new responsibilities as a result of the new relationship you could ask for any maintenance payments to be reduced. All the same, your responsibility to maintain your former spouse will always take precedence over your new commitments.

It may also be worth noting that if you start cohabiting with a new partner, then your right to maintenance, at least at the same level as you have been receiving it, may be challenged. Your right to remain in the marital home may also be affected, but that will depend on the terms of the divorce.

---

*"Financial concerns are not often at the forefront of your mind when you remarry, particularly when you are not having to buy a house. All the same some policy decisions about things like presents and family outings might prevent unease later on."*

---

## PARENTING AND STEP-PARENTING

The law relating to children has undergone a serious overhaul in the last few years. The aim of the Children Act 1989 was to provide a consistent and comprehensive code of law which swept away the piecemeal and sometimes contradictory legislation which had been amassed over the decades.

The emphasis is now clearly on the rights and needs of the child rather than the parent. For a start, the new laws changed some of the familiar old terms. Parental rights and duties are now referred to as parental responsibilities. Access orders have become contact orders and legal custody and custodianship have been replaced by residence orders.

In any disputes about children, the court's primary consideration will be the welfare of the child. In fact, if the court has been asked by parents, guardians or the local authority to take certain steps that will affect the child, it will only do so if it thinks the outcome will be better than not taking any steps at all.

The term step-parent currently has little legal significance in its own right.

As a step-parent you take on certain responsibilities towards the day-to-day welfare of your stepchildren in the same way that a nanny or grandparent takes responsibility for a child in their temporary care.

In addition, you might take on an obligation to maintain a

stepchild who has lived with you as part of your family. In practical terms this could mean that a dependent stepchild could make a claim against your estate after your death. You may also be asked to pay maintenance if you split up from the child's birth parent. Equally, you may be able to apply for maintenance for a stepchild left in your care.

Step-parents have no automatic parental rights. Unless you take steps to acquire parental rights and responsibilities by, for example, adopting the child, becoming its legal guardian or being granted a residence order, you will have no jurisdiction over your stepchild. This means that you cannot take decisions about the child's life, such as which school they attend, whether they submit to medical treatment or their religious upbringing. Strictly speaking, you also have no say in arguments over less fundamental but more trying issues like hair cuts, ear piercing and girl/boyfriends.

The terms parental responsibilities, residence orders and so on are explained in greater detail on the following pages. Issues relating to child maintenance are dealt with on pages 82–87.

## In and out of wedlock

With the increasing social acceptance of cohabitation and lone motherhood, the stigma associated with illegitimacy has all but disappeared. However, the law continues to make a distinction between children born to parents who are married and children born to parents who are unmarried. As a nod to modernity, legislation now attempts to avoid labelling children as legitimate or illegitimate by referring to the marital status of the parents instead of the birth status of the children.

Basically the law regards children as legitimate if they are conceived or born while their parents are married. This means they are legitimate if their parents were:

- married at the time of conception but divorce before the child is born.
- cohabiting at the time of conception but marry before the child is born.

A child who was born illegitimate and is then adopted will be regarded as the legitimate child of its adoptive parents.

## From illegitimate to legitimate

Even if a child is born illegitimate because their parents weren't married either at their conception or birth, they can still achieve legitimate status. This process is known as legitimation. There are three ways to legitimate a child:

- The parents subsequently marry – even if they were married to other partners at the time the child was born.

  *Gillian and Eddie had an affair while they were both married to other partners. Gillian became pregnant and left her husband, taking their two children with her. She moved in with Eddie, whose wife had by then gone off with someone else. Gillian's husband was difficult over the divorce and it took over five years before a decree absolute was granted. In the meantime Gillian and Eddie's daughter, Carrie, was born. They were finally free to marry on Carrie's sixth birthday, which was the point at which she became legitimate.*

- The child is adopted jointly by the mother and her husband (who is not the child's father), as in a typical stepfamily adoption (see page 63).
- The child is adopted by the mother alone. This is usually only possible if the father is dead or missing or there is some very good reason for excluding him from the child's future.

You cannot legitimate a child simply by putting their father's name on their birth certificate.

Although a legitimated child has almost the same rights as if they had been born legitimate, some differences remain, especially when it comes to property and inheritance rights. When the right to inherit depends on the relative seniority of the children, the legitimated child ranks as if they had been born on the date of legitimation. This is why in stepfamilies it is important not to rely on chronological birth dates when, for example, writing a will (see page 121).

## Birth certificates and names

When both parents are married one or other of them will register the birth. Unmarried fathers, on the other hand, are not obliged to register their children and have no independent right to have their name entered on the register. Unmarried mothers can only enter the father's name if they both agree and sign the register, they each produce sworn statements, or they have an appropriate court order.

Although it is customary for children to take their father's surname, there's no requirement to do this. Remember that you cannot unilaterally decide to change a child's name without the other parent's consent. In most cases it's extremely difficult to change names even after a divorce. A stepchild can only take on the name of their step-parent with the consent of both birth parents, or the agreement of the court, or through adoption.

## Stepchildren and name changing

Name changing is a big issue for many stepfamilies, especially those with quite young children. However, you need to think very carefully about the possible consequences. Obviously where one birth parent is dead there may be fewer considerations. Here are the pros and cons of name changing:

*Pros*

- Reinforces the notion of a new and coherent family unit.
- All the children have the same surname, which is easier to manage at school etc.
- Loses any stigma you may have felt as a divorcing family or a lone parent family.

*Cons*

- May force a sense of togetherness when children are still coming to terms with the idea of a new family.
- Could cause division between siblings where they are not all in the same day-to-day family unit.
- The child loses identity with the non-resident parent.
- The child may resent it in later life when they want to reassert their identity with the non-resident parent.

Those are some of the emotional considerations. Above all you need to be realistic about the legal position.

You cannot simply change a child's surname when you remarry or set up a new partnership without consulting the other birth parent. Where there is a residence order in effect, you will first need to seek the written consent of everyone with parental responsibility for that child or the consent of the court. The court would be very reluctant to let a change of name go ahead unless it could be persuaded that it was in the child's best interests.

## Parental responsibilities

The law doesn't actually list the rights and duties of parents, but current practice suggests what is and isn't acceptable. Generally, anyone caring for a child, whether a parent, step-parent or guardian, is expected to look after and maintain the child. If they fail to do so the child may be removed from their care and they may be liable to prosecution. Parental power is not sacrosanct and if the courts believe that a carer's actions will damage the child in some way then they will intervene.

### Who takes responsibility

If the child's parents were married to each other at the time the child was conceived or born, or the child is subsequently legitimated, then both parents have parental responsibility.

If the parents are unmarried then parental responsibility rests solely with the mother. Although an unmarried father can take steps to acquire parental responsibility, he has no automatic rights to this. It's important to note that even if the unmarried father has taken steps to acquire parental responsibility, it can be terminated.

Apart from the child's parents other people can acquire parental responsibility, for example by getting a residence order, becoming a guardian or through adoption.

As a parent you can never give up parental responsibility even if other people acquire it as well. Parental responsibility will only be lost if your child is adopted.

### Step-parents and parental responsibility

Whatever you consider to be your day-to-day responsibilities towards your stepchildren, as far as the law is concerned you have no more rights than, say, a childminder or the parent of one of your stepchild's friends. This means that while you have a duty to ensure the child is fed and watered every day and kept out of harm's way while in your care, you cannot make any significant decisions about their life.

If you want to formalise your relationship with your step children, then you have two options. You can either acquire parental responsibility by way of a residence order (see below) or you can adopt the child jointly with their natural parent (see page 63).

There is a proposal to amend current legislation in order to allow a step-parent to acquire parental responsibility in a similar way to an unmarried father. To a great extent this will get round the need for step-parents to apply to adopt a stepchild.

## Residence orders

Even if you are granted a residence order, you still won't exercise the same degree of parental responsibility over your stepchild as you would over your birth child. For example, you couldn't appoint a guardian for the stepchild or agree to give them up for adoption. In addition, other special restrictions may be applied. In any case, parental responsibility granted by the courts will come to an end when the child reaches 16 unless there are very special circumstances.

As a step-parent you can ask for a residence order provided that one of the following applies:

- You are a partner in a marriage in which the stepchild is regarded as a child of the family. You can apply even if this marriage has now been dissolved.

- Your stepchild has lived with you for at least three years. The three-year period doesn't need to be continuous, but it must not have begun more than five years before and it must not have ended more than three months before you make the application.

- You have the agreement of the person who currently has a residence order or, if the child is in local authority care, the consent of that authority.

- You have the consent of each of those (if any) who already have parental responsibility for the child.

To make an application for a residence order you should apply in the first instance to your local Magistrates Court.

## Adoption

Traditionally adoption has been seen as the preserve of childless couples. The availability of both contraception and legal abortion, together with the increasing acceptance of lone motherhood, have meant that now very few babies are adopted each year. Adoptions today tend to focus on finding families for children with special needs. More than half of adoptions are of children aged five and over. What's more significant is that around half of all adoptions are by step-parents.

Once a child is adopted the birth parent(s) relinquish all parental rights. However, if you oppose your child's being put up for adoption then you can take steps to try and stop the process. You should take legal advice about what to do.

Prospective adopters fall into two categories: those who are unrelated to the child and those who are directly related, usually the parents.

If you are unrelated to the child you want to adopt, you have to be over 21 and domiciled in Britain. Normally only one half of a cohabiting couple may apply. The adoption process is strictly regulated and you will have to go through an adoption agency who may impose other restrictions such as age limits and health requirements. The agency will help you through the legal process.

### Related adopters

There are usually two sets of circumstances where a related adult might want to adopt a child.

### Parent and step-parent

A parent, whether or not they were married when they had the child, may later marry or remarry and wish to adopt their child with their new spouse.

The court's major concern will be about the child's relationship with the absent parent, usually the father. They will be reluctant to take any steps which will sever that relationship without very good cause. Providing the step-parent is over 21, the birth parent need only be 18 to go ahead with this type of adoption.

From a legal point of view, adoption enables the strongest relationship between step-parent and stepchild. However, it's not something that should be undertaken lightly. The effect of adoption is to sever absolutely the child's legal ties to one or both of its birth parents. This means that the birth parent no longer has parental responsibility for the child. It also means that the child loses all its rights in respect of the parent. In particular, from a financial point of view they lose their inheritance rights. They also lose contact with an entire network of family members. In addition they may lose their right to inherit from their birth grandparents, aunts, uncles and so on.

Most courts will be extremely reluctant to grant an adoption order where one of the birth parents is still alive unless there is a very good reason for the child to lose all contact with that parent. They will also be concerned about the relationship with other family members, for example, grandparents. The court is likely to dismiss an application for adoption by a parent and step-parent if they think the issue could be dealt with more constructively by, for example, using residence and contact orders.

### Mother or unmarried father

If the mother or unmarried father applies individually to adopt the child, the court will not make an adoption order unless it is satisfied that the other parent cannot be found or there is some other good reason to exclude the latter from the child's upbringing.

If the child's mother dies, an unmarried father can apply to the court to adopt his child. The result of the adoption order will mean that he assumes all parental responsibilities and the child will become legitimate.

Unmarried couples will not be able jointly to adopt their child. Adoption orders will usually only be granted to applicants who are married to each other, for example parent and step-parent.

## Children on the move

One of the facets of stepfamily life is that parents and children can live in a fairly fluid family unit. Children may be full-time or part-time stepchildren and their status may change as time goes on. To a great extent this won't affect your long-term financial planning. However, it may well affect your benefit entitlement and you will probably need to adjust your monthly budget. If your family arrangements change significantly you should think about the following:

- Will your entitlement to child benefit change? Child benefit will be paid to the person with whom the child lives (see page 133).

- How will the child's move affect any maintenance that you are either paying or receiving? Do you need to have the court order/assessment varied?

- If your maintenance payments are changed, how will this affect your tax position?

- Will you need to apply for means-tested benefits? Any request for benefits will immediately trigger a Child Support Agency assessment.

- Do you need to change who receives the additional personal allowance (see page 156)?

# BREAKING RELATIONSHIPS

The legal system provides a number of ways of ending a marriage, either on a temporary basis or for good. The path you decide to follow will depend on the state of your current relationship, any previous experience you've had of splitting up and also on your financial situation. For the majority of couples there are two distinct parts to the business of splitting up. The first is about unravelling your legal ties. The second deals with untangling your financial affairs. The following pages explain the legal process. To find out more about the financial split, start on page 70.

The position of cohabitees is very different. You can find out about ending a live-in relationship on page 78.

## Easing the trauma of a break-up

However amicable the split, separation and divorce hurt – emotionally and financially. The fallout from an acrimonious divorce can last for an eternity and affect any number of subsequent relationships.

For the sake of your pocket and your sanity, and in particular the well-being of your children and any stepchildren, it's in everybody's interests to make the process of breaking up as civilised and businesslike as possible. Having said that, it is very difficult to remain cool and detached throughout what is a very personal and often painful process.

There are two ways in which you can help yourself and your family towards a more productive and positive separation. The first is to seek the help of a professional conciliator or family mediator. Their aim is to help you manage the business of breaking up by reducing conflict and looking at the various practical options open to you. In this way you can stave off escalating legal costs. The conciliator or mediator provides a neutral space where you and your partner can try and come to an agreement about your home, your money and care for your children.

Don't confuse conciliation with the reconciliation services offered by organisations such as Relate. Reconciliation may help you to resolve your differences and cement the family unit. Conciliation starts from the premise that the relationship has already dissolved – although of course it won't preclude a reconciliation. There are independent conciliation services throughout the country and you can obtain details of what's available in your area through National Family Mediation (for address see page 178).

Second, try and instruct a solicitor who belongs to the Solicitors' Family Law Association. Once again, their aim is to make the legal process as free as possible from conflict and antagonism. Their objective is to reach sound and reasonable agreements as quickly as possible without indulging in unnecessary blood letting. Do not go for the school of 'I'll get him for every penny' solicitors – you really don't need anyone to stoke unnecessary fires for you.

However tempting it might seem at the time, there are absolutely no long-term benefits to be gained by turning the separation process into a battlefield. The repercussions from such a strategy may well take their toll on the well-being of the family – both new and existing units – far into the future.

**Watch out!** If you have very little money you may be entitled to help with your legal costs through the means-tested Legal Aid and Advice Scheme. You may qualify for help under the Green Form Scheme in order to complete the necessary divorce procedure forms. You won't be entitled to full legal aid in an undefended divorce. You may, however, get full legal aid in order to be represented at custody or maintenance hearings. Remember too that if you are seeking help with your legal costs, only your own income, not your spouse's, will count for the purposes of the legal aid calculations. If, however, you are living with a new partner, then their income may affect the calculations and your entitlement.

## The break-up options

### Judicial separation

Although rarely used these days, judicial separation does give legal recognition and financial protection to people unable or unwilling to get divorced. A judicial separation ends your obligation to live with your spouse, but it does not end your marriage and therefore you cannot remarry.

However, you may be left in a state of limbo with regard to certain financial matters. You can obtain a lump sum payment as well as maintenance on the final application of the judicial separation proceedings. Because the marriage is not actually dissolved a wife may be entitled to receive any widow's pension if her husband dies. However, should either partner die without making a will, then the survivor will not be treated as a spouse under the intestacy rules (see page 125). Nevertheless, they may be able to make a claim under the Inheritance

Act (see page 126). For these reasons you should obtain advice before opting for a judicial separation.

Obtaining a judicial separation is much the same as getting a divorce (see below) except that you don't have to prove that the marriage has broken down irretrievably.

### Annulment

In order to have your marriage annulled you have to prove one of two things. Either that it is void – it never legally existed – for example because one or both partners was under age or already married; or else that the marriage was legal but voidable because it has never been consummated.

Once a decree of nullity is granted because the marriage is void, it is as if the wedding had never taken place in law. However, any children would remain legitimate.

### Separation agreements

You can also signal the end of your relationship by drawing up a separation agreement but this in itself does not bring about the legal end to your marriage. Separation agreements focus on the financial split and can also deal with other aspects of the relationship, for example arrangements for the children. These are dealt with in greater detail on page 73.

### Divorce

Divorce is the ultimate marital U-turn, the point of no return. If you want to get back together with your ex, then you will have to remarry. In order to start proceedings you must prove three facts:

1. That the marriage is valid – your marriage certificate should suffice.
2. That you've been married for at least a year.
3. That you or your spouse has been either legally domiciled – regard this as your permanent home – or resident in England or Wales for at least a year before starting divorce proceedings.

In addition, you must also show that the marriage has broken down irretrievably. This is the only ground for divorce and there are five ways of proving it:

1   <u>Adultery</u>. You have to show that not only has your spouse committed adultery but that in addition you find it intolerable to continue living with them.

2. <u>Unreasonable behaviour</u>. This means that your spouse has behaved in such a way that you cannot be expected to live with them.

3. <u>Desertion</u>. Your spouse left you, against your will and without good reason, at least two years ago.

4. <u>Two years' separation with consent</u>. You and your spouse have lived apart for at least two years and both of you agree to the divorce.

5. <u>Five years' separation without consent</u>. You and your spouse have lived apart for a continuous period of at least five years.

**Law watch!** There are proposals to amend the divorce process fundamentally. The aim is to introduce 'no fault divorce' by doing away with divorce based on adultery or unreasonable behaviour, which couples often use to bypass the two-year divorce by consent period. There will also be a one-year wait between making an initial statement and applying for the divorce decree. In addition, there will be a greater emphasis on family mediation as part of the divorce procedure.

## The divorce procedure

There are three parts to getting divorced. The first concerns the legal process of dissolving the contract you entered into when you got married. The second deals with financial matters. The third looks at how children will be cared for and how they will be supported. Invariably there is a good deal of overlap between parts two and three. The following paragraphs look at dissolving the marriage contract. More information about divorce and money can be found on page 70. Information on children and divorce starts on page 79.

**Watch out!** As explained above, divorce is not a single procedure. When you start divorce proceedings you will put in motion a number of different processes – legal, financial and those to do with children. Although they usually begin together, they may end up progressing at different paces.

### Undefended divorce

Almost all divorces are undefended – not contested. Since arrangements about finances and children are made separately, you can still go ahead with an undefended divorce even if you cannot agree what to do about money or the kids. As a result, the majority of straightforward divorces are dealt with by Special Procedure. This means that even if you have children you may never need to step foot inside a court.

### Filling in the forms

The undefended divorce procedure is relatively simple to follow and there's nothing to stop you doing it yourself. You'll first need to get an application form or petition from your local Divorce County Court or the Divorce Registry if you live in London – look for their addresses in the telephone directory.

Once completed you'll need to send the form together with a copy of your marriage certificate and the court fee back to the court. The petition is sent on to your spouse, who is known as the respondent, and they must reply to it. If the respondent doesn't intend to contest the divorce then you'll need to complete an Affidavit under the Special Procedure to back up your original petition and ask for your case to be decided by a District Judge. The affidavit – a sworn statement – is in a simple question and answer format.

Providing the judge is satisfied that there is sufficient evidence to support your petition you will be granted a decree nisi or interim decree. Six weeks later you can apply for a decree absolute, which means that your marriage is officially ended. If the petitioner fails to apply within three months then the respondent can do so instead. The court will only grant the final order once it is happy about the arrangements for the children.

### Defended divorce

Defending a divorce is expensive and often fruitless. Most defended petitions are settled out of court, usually after large sums of money have been expended on legal fees. Denying that the marriage has broken down irretrievably may delay the divorce, but it's unlikely to put it off for ever if the petitioner is determined to go through with it.

If you disagree with the grounds given for divorce you can cross-pray – petition for divorce on different grounds. Provided that your spouse doesn't object you can still go for the undefended procedure.

# The financial break-up

This section looks at the powers of the court to determine what happens to your home, money and other assets when you split up. It explains the different types of orders the courts can make, the sort of things they take into consideration when making their judgments, and how you can vary and enforce their decisions. The information on these pages is relevant to spousal maintenance. Financial provision for children is explained separately on page 82. This is because most child maintenance is now dealt with by the Child Support Agency and not by the courts. However, there are instances, where for example you want to apply for maintenance for a stepchild, where you will still need to go through the court system. The CSA does not handle these types of special cases.

**WATCH OUT!**

**Watch out!** If you are seeking financial provision for your children then this will be dealt with by the Child Support Agency (CSA) (see page 82). For the time being this will not affect those parents who are already divorced, unless you do not already have a court order for child maintenance or you rely on State benefits. However, eventually the new procedures will encompass all separating and divorcing parents. It is still not entirely clear how the courts and the CSA will ultimately interrelate in terms of determining the overall financial break-up. The most important thing to bear in mind is that the CSA will in effect be able to override the practice of 'clean break' agreements made after April 1993. This means that if you agree to give your spouse the marital home in exchange for no or limited maintenance for your children, you may find yourself required by the CSA at some later date to increase your maintenance provision. Anyone who is in the process of separating and finds themselves in this position should seek expert legal help.

## Court orders

Basically the courts can make two categories of financial order: financial provision orders which are about income, and property adjustment orders which are to do with the family's capital assets.

### Financial provision orders

There are three types of order:

- <u>Maintenance orders</u>: orders for periodical payments from one spouse to the other, usually on a weekly or monthly basis. The amount awarded is designed to cover living expenses. This kind of order will no longer be payable if either of the partners dies or the recipient remarries.

- Secured periodical payments: some assets are put aside and invested in order to produce income to pay one spouse. If the recipient remarries or dies then the assets may return to the payer. However, the payments will not necessarily end if the payer dies.
- Lump sum payments: one spouse pays the other a substantial once-and-for-all lump sum. However, the lump sum can be paid in instalments. This idea is much favoured by the courts because it provides a 'clean break' approach to what might otherwise be a lingering divorce settlement. However, it remains to be seen whether the impact of the Child Support Act will drive out these kind of settlements for couples with dependent children.

**Property adjustment orders**

The court has the power to decide how to allocate property between spouses. In reaching a decision its aim is not just to try and ensure that the allocation reflects the contributions – both financial and otherwise – that both spouses have put into acquiring and maintaining their home and their lifestyle. They also want to see that both parties, and especially any dependent children, have a roof over their head on the other side of the divorce.

However, this is not always a simple task. For a start, there just may not be enough capital in the home to enable both spouses to purchase a home of their own. Secondly, the court needs to consider whether, if one spouse remains in the family home, they will have enough income to maintain it.

To achieve a settlement the court can order one spouse to transfer the home into the other spouse's name or to sell it and divide up the profits. Alternatively it may allow the parent with a residence order to remain in the property until the children have grown up. Again, we will need to wait and see how the Child Support Act will affect the trend in property adjustment orders.

**When to apply to the courts for financial help**

You don't need to wait until you have started the divorce ball rolling to get help to sort out your finances. In fact, you can ask the courts to make you a financial order during a trial separation, even if you and your spouse eventually get back together.

**Before starting divorce proceedings**

You have a number of options. You can come to an informal

agreement or you can draw up a separation agreement (see page 73). You can also ask the court for a maintenance order.

You can apply for maintenance orders in the Magistrates Court or the County Court. In very special circumstances you can apply to the High Court. The County Court has more extensive powers than the Magistrates Court.

**Watch out!** If you have any concerns about your immediate financial welfare, for example your spouse running off with the family silver or disposing of valuable assets, contact a solicitor without delay

### During divorce proceedings

Once you have submitted the divorce petition then you can apply for financial relief through the Divorce County court. This can be for yourself and any stepchild who has been treated as part of the family, and, in very special circumstances, a birth child (see page 87). The CSA rather than the courts now deals with financial provision for birth children unless there is an application for substantial additional maintenance, for example to pay school fees. It doesn't matter which of you filed for divorce, both the petitioner and the respondent can ask for financial help.

Orders made at this stage cannot provide any long-term solutions about ongoing maintenance or who gets the family home – those can only come into effect when the decree absolute is granted. You can apply for immediate financial help any time from when the divorce proceedings begin up until the time the divorce is made absolute.

Since an order can only be temporary it is known as maintenance pending suit; in other words, maintenance while the divorce is being decided. If the District Judge is unable to make an immediate decision about the amount of maintenance to be granted, they can make an even more temporary order called interim maintenance.

### Long-term solutions

Even if you have undertaken your own undefended divorce, you ought to get professional legal help before embarking on a claim for financial relief or a property adjustment order. Although you can apply for long-term financial settlements as soon as you begin the divorce proceedings, the court won't finalise them until your decree nisi has been granted.

Both husband and wife can apply to the court whether they are the petitioner or respondent. The petitioner completes a form known as a 'notice of intention to proceed with application for ancillary relief made in petition'. The respondent applies by 'notice of application for ancillary relief'.

You will need to complete three copies of the forms. You will also need to supply an affidavit or sworn statement to support your application.

At this stage you should think carefully about each and every claim you might want to make in the future – you won't need to set down specific amounts of money. If you don't do this, you could discover later that you have under-calculated your needs and you may find it difficult to amend your request. This isn't about 'getting one over' on your partner. It's just very important to remember that you are establishing your financial future and it's best to lay all your needs on the table at the start.

If your spouse appears unwilling to co-operate and respond to your application, ask the court for help immediately. Don't worry if you're unhappy with the information your spouse has supplied to the court, you will have the opportunity to challenge it.

The stage-by-stage court procedure for assessing financial provision gives both spouses ample opportunity to try and reach an amicable settlement without resorting to what could be an extremely expensive final court hearing. However, if you continue to dispute how to divide up your property then you will have to proceed to a hearing. You should not attempt this without proper legal advice. As always, it's much better if, with the help of your solicitor or a mediator, you can agree between yourselves.

## Separation agreements

At its most basic a separation agreement can be a simple informal agreement written by a husband and wife setting out how they want to deal with their financial affairs. To carry any weight it ought to be drawn up by a solicitor and properly witnessed and signed. Such an agreement is a useful tool during a two-year separation. It enables you to sort out your affairs, so that the agreement forms the basis for the final court order at the end of the divorce proceedings (see below).

### Informal agreements

Separation agreements work well on an informal basis if both spouses are on amicable terms and can agree on how to settle their finances. They are also useful as an interim measure before you start divorce proceedings or during a trial separation. Although the advantage of this kind of agreement is that you don't have to go to court, the court can overrule it if negotiations break down or one partner feels they have been unfairly treated.

In drawing up an agreement you must remember that you cannot prevent your spouse from applying to the court at a later date to review your financial settlement. You also cannot use a separation agreement to make binding arrangements about financial provision for your children.

### Varying the agreement

A separation agreement may end if you both decide to terminate it or if one person breaks the terms of the agreement and the other seeks redress through the courts. The agreement will also come to an end if one of you dies or remarries. In this situation what will happen will depend on the original terms of the agreement.

### Separation agreements and divorce proceedings

At its most formal the contents of a separation agreement can be embodied in a court order. If you want to use your separation agreement as the basis for your final divorce settlement, you can do this by asking for something called a consent order from the court. In this case both parties will be asked to submit a summary of their individual financial situations.

## Enforcing court orders

Having a financial award made is one thing; getting your spouse to pay up may be altogether another. The remedy open to you will depend on the type of order made and which court made it.

---

*"I used to feel very angry that I only got maintenance*
*when I threatened court action.*
*It was always in arrears and only paid on the threat of*
*prison which made me look like a bully.*
*My second husband would have been prepared to forgo*
*the maintenance I received had it meant that all contact*
*and harassment would stop. But it wouldn't have and*
*he felt we all deserved the money.*
*The lack of maintenance made everyone angry as*
*it limited money for holidays, treats –*
*anything extra like special clothes or hobbies."*

---

### Maintenance defaulters

The Divorce Court has three ways to attempt to make reluctant spouses pay maintenance:

1. If the recalcitrant spouse is an employee, the court can issue an attachment of earnings order. This means that your spouse's employer will be ordered to deduct regular weekly or monthly amounts from their pay, which will be sent to the court in order to cover the outstanding maintenance.

2. If you can show that your spouse has the means to pay you maintenance but has refused to do so, then you can ask the court to issue a judgment summons for committal to prison. Usually the threat of such extreme action has the desired effect. However, you should not undertake this lightly and you'll need a solicitor's advice.

3. It can issue a warrant of execution. Not as drastic as it might sound! It simply means the court can order the bailiffs to seize sufficient of the defaulter's goods to pay off the arrears.

### Problems with lump sum and property adjustment orders

If your ex-spouse fails to pay up then you could start bankruptcy proceedings – although this might prove fruitless. Or you can ask the court to order your spouse to sell any property they were awarded under the financial settlement – such as a house or shares – in order to raise the money to pay the lump sum.

Where an ex-spouse fails to comply with a property adjustment order the court can carry out the relevant conveyancing procedure itself. If you find yourself in this situation, ask for a solicitor's help.

## Varying court orders

Apart from lump sum and property adjustment orders, any other orders relating to finances can be varied if your circumstances change. Although you can't vary the total amount of a lump sum payment, you may be able to vary the amount of the instalments by which it's paid.

What you can't do is go back to the court at a later stage and automatically obtain a different order if you didn't ask for it in your original application. By the same token, if your claim for maintenance was dismissed initially, you are unlikely to be able to revive it later on. However, if your spouse gave inaccurate or misleading information originally, then you may be able to re-apply.

There are all sorts of reasons why you might want to vary the terms of an order. For example your circumstances might change –

you might retire or lose your job; the person receiving the money may remarry or cohabit, in which case the payments will cease; the payer may remarry or cohabit; either of you might become disabled or die.

In order to vary an order you will have to re-apply to the court using a standard form.

### Remarriage and cohabitation

If you remarry then any spousal maintenance payments you receive cease immediately. You cannot revive them if you later get divorced or your new partner dies. You do not have to notify your ex-spouse formally of your change in circumstances. However, if they find out they will be entitled to apply to the court for you to repay any maintenance they've given you since you remarried. If you refuse to return the cash they can sue you for the debt. This does not affect any lump sum or property adjustment orders.

If your ex-spouse remarries very soon after your divorce and you've paid out thousands in a lump sum or agreed to a property adjustment order, there's usually not much you can do about it. In very rare cases you may be able to have the order set aside, for example if your former spouse intended to remarry or else concealed huge assets. If you're paying the lump sum by instalments, you'll have to continue paying up even if your ex is now happily ensconced with a new partner.

If either partner starts cohabiting with someone else you may be able to vary the order. However, if you're the one doing the paying out, your obligations to your former spouse will still take priority.

---

*"Maintenance was a difficult issue. We felt grudging about giving his ex-wife money for herself since she had left my second husband. However, we didn't want to stint the children so it was a delicate balance."*

---

### Variation on death

If the recipient dies then the payer stops making maintenance payments. However, any outstanding instalments of a lump sum order will have to be paid to the deceased's estate.

If the payer dies then once again maintenance payments will usually cease. Unless the court has expressly forbidden it, the surviving ex-spouse should immediately apply to the court for financial provision out of the deceased's estate.

## How the court makes a decision

The court will take into account all the circumstances of the divorcing couple. However, the welfare of any dependent children will always be its first consideration. (For more information about children and divorce settlements, see page 79).

In particular the court will consider the following:

- The income and potential earning capacity of each spouse. The court cannot order anyone to take a job, but they will look at whether either spouse can reasonably be expected to increase what they earn. Obviously the court recognises the limitations, say, of an older woman approaching retirement who's never worked, or a mother responsible for looking after young children.

  However, if the court thinks you – or your spouse – are deliberately avoiding work or taking a lower-paid job in order to claim or wriggle out of paying maintenance, then it will deem you to have a level of income. This means that it will base its settlement calculations on the earning capacity which it thinks you could achieve.

- The property and other financial resources of each spouse, particularly in the foreseeable future.

- The financial needs, obligation and responsibilities of each person. The court will also consider the family's standard of living before the marriage broke up. In addition, the mental and physical welfare of each partner will be taken into account.

- The length of the marriage. Basically the rule seems to be the shorter the marriage the more likely you are to receive only whatever you put in, particularly if you're young and childless.

- Whether either spouse is about to embark on a fresh relationship. Moving in with a new partner may lower your outgoings, but equally it may bring new financial burdens. A new partner cannot be required to contribute towards maintaining their cohabitee's former family. However, a new partner may be asked to supply the court with brief details about their financial arrangements regarding support for the divorcing spouse.

- Pension rights and possible welfare benefit losses. Pension rights on divorce is one of the current political hot potatoes and there are proposals to bring in more equitable settlements. From April 1996, the provisions of the Pension Act 1995 means that courts throughout the UK will be required to take pension rights into account when making financial provision orders in divorce settlements. In addition, the court currently has to consider whether

one spouse will lose the right to claim benefits, for example a widow's pension, as a result of the divorce, and they may decide to compensate for this.

Finally, the court will also take into account the conduct of each spouse, but usually only if this is relevant to the financial issues involved.

## Ending a cohabiting relationship

In theory you can just walk away with no marital cords to be cut. In practice, if you've been living 'as man and wife' you've probably taken on the trappings of a regular wedded couple with all the complexities that go with entangling two or more lives.

If you cannot agree how to unravel your lives, then ultimately you can turn to the court for help. However, unlike married couples, the court does not have the same discretion to redistribute the family wealth. In dividing up your home, money and other assets the following principles will apply:

- The only person or people entitled to continue living in the home – or to benefit from the sale of it – are those who legally own the property. It is extremely difficult to prove an interest in a property where no written agreement exists (see page 142).
- If you both legally own the property and one of you refuses to agree to sell it or to let the other buy them out, then the court can order a sale.
- If you don't legally own your home but you have a beneficial interest in the property (see page 141) then you will be entitled to some of the profit on the sale of the home, if there is any. However, since your partner could sell the property without your consent – or even knowledge – you should take steps to protect your interest (see page 142).
- Any savings accounts or other assets which are in your sole name are yours alone. The same applies to any belongings you brought with you into the relationship, anything you bought with your own money, or items and gifts that were given to you personally.
- Any savings or other assets which are in your joint names will probably be regarded as a common purse and divided up equally, regardless who how much each of you contributed in the first place. The only exception is where you have drawn up a trust deed stating that a particular sum of money or valuable item belongs to one person only.

## Children of separating parents

Once again, there are two parts to the process of separation and divorce. The first is the legal disentangling, which as far as children are concerned has to do with who will look after them when their parents split up. The second part is about financial provision.

The most fundamental change for separating parents has been the introduction of the Child Support Act 1991. This has radically shaken up the way child maintenance is assessed and collected. Because the Act is still new, it's very difficult to tell the extent of its decision-making powers. Both the Act and the Child Support Agency (CSA), its administrative arm, are under constant review (and under fire). For this reason, this chapter explains only the principles of the workings of the Act and the CSA.

**Watch out!** If you are a step-parent you may retain a duty to maintain your stepchildren, even if your relationship with their birth parent is over. If the stepchild has lived with you as part of your family – eaten with you and slept under the same roof – then they may be able to make a claim against you for maintenance. By the same token, if you continue to care for a stepchild whose birth parent has left the relationship, you can make a claim against them for maintenance for the stepchild.

WATCH OUT!

### The legal arrangements

If you cohabit or you're married but don't want to go through the process of divorce, then you can agree informally about who cares for your children and the status of the non-resident parent (see page 61). You can also come to an informal agreement about maintenance. You may wish to see a solicitor and get them to draw up a proper document for you. Do remember though that either parent, married or not, can apply to the court or the Child Support Agency for a maintenance assessment. As a result you may have to formalise your care arrangements through the court.

If you are in the process of divorcing, then you will find that the court will have to be satisfied about your arrangements for the care of your children before they will grant a decree absolute.

Whatever your marital status, if you cannot agree about what happens to your children when you separate, the court will decide for you. If you are in dispute you should seek the advice of a solicitor.

### Court orders

In addition to orders for maintenance, the court can make two main types of order to do with the care of children: residence orders which state with whom the child will live, and contact orders which state the child's access to another named person. However, the court won't make any orders unless it is in the child's interests to do so.

The new orders are intended to offer far more flexibility than the old notion of custody and access. Both types of order will end when the child reaches 16 unless there are special circumstances, for example the child is mentally or physically disabled.

The law lays down who can actually apply for a residence or contact order. These include:

- the child's parent, married or unmarried, step-parent or former step-parent,
- the child's guardian,
- anyone with whom the child has lived for at least three years. This doesn't have to be the three years immediately preceding the application, so long as it's not more than five years previously,
- anyone who applies with the consent of those who currently have parental responsibility for the child.

Other people may be able to apply in certain special circumstances.

### *Residence orders*

Residence orders can be granted in favour of more than one person, thus enabling the child to live with both parents. Once you are granted a residence order you automatically get parental responsibility even if you don't already have it (see page 61). This will last for as long as the order is in force. Granting a residence order to one parent or to someone other than the parents will not remove parental responsibility from either of the birth parents.

However, there will still be restrictions on what you can and cannot do. For example, unless you are the parent or the legal guardian of the child, you will not be able to free the child for adoption, appoint a guardian, change their name or take the child out of the country for more than one month.

### *Contact orders*

The old 'access order' has been reworded to emphasise the concept of the child's right to contact with their parent and not the other way around. A contact order requires the person with whom the child is living to allow the child to have contact with the person named on the order. That person, however, is not compelled to have contact with the child.

*Susie and Jim split up. Susie is awarded a residence order for their child, Dora. Jim applies for a contact order, which he is granted. Despite Susie and Dora's efforts to maintain the relationship, Jim later decides he has no wish to keep any contact with his daughter. Apart from continuing to pay maintenance, the court cannot compel him to have anything more to do with his daughter.*

### Other orders

There are also two other types of order that you might come across:

- A prohibited steps order prevents the person who cares for the child from doing certain things such as taking the child out of the country.

- A specific issue order addresses a particular problem or dispute that might arise in connection with parental responsibility.

### How the court decides

Unlike the new CSA rules for calculating financial provision, the court has no hard and fast rules for deciding how a child is cared for when a relationship breaks up. Each case is judged on its own merits; however, there are some guiding principles. The court will take into consideration the following factors:

- The need for stability. The court will be keen to ensure that the child experiences as little upheaval as possible. For this reason they tend to be reluctant to remove a child from the parent who is currently caring for them, provided that the relationship appears happy and settled. The court may also be reticent about splitting up siblings.

- The child's views. Courts are encouraged to take into consideration the views and wishes of the children involved. However, most judges will be alert to the fact that children may have been primed by one parent or the other.

- Although the material benefits of each parent will be considered, they are unlikely to be the deciding factor. The quality of day-to-day care is far more important than whether you live in a high-rise flat or a semi in the suburbs.

- The parents' behaviour. The court isn't interested in who, if any-one, 'caused' the break-up, unless it had or has a direct effect on the welfare of the child.

*Three years ago Melanie started having an affair with a man she met through work. They would only meet at lunchtimes and none of the family knew about it until a jealous colleague spilt the beans to Melanie's husband, Jeff. The fact that Melanie had an affair does not make her unsuitable to retain care of her children.*

*However, if, for example, Jeff had been away from home for long periods and during that time Melanie had used her home for a series of drunken orgies, then the court may well consider her behaviour as critical to their decision.*

### The procedure

When you complete the divorce petition you must also complete a 'statement as to arrangements for children'. The respondent will need to reply in much the same way as to the divorce petition (see page 69). In most cases and where there is no dispute you will get approval for the arrangements, but in some instances you may be asked to supply further information and you may need to go to court. Once this has been satisfied you will get a copy of the official order enabling you to apply for the decree nisi to be made absolute.

If you cannot agree about the arrangements for your children, then you must seek the help of a solicitor. Remember, any kind of legal wrangle will be time consuming and could be extremely expensive. More than that, it will not help your children and stepchildren deal with the inevitable upset that a separation creates (see page 65).

Court orders are designed to be long term and you cannot challenge them just because you don't like what the judge has decided. However, if you have genuine concerns about the welfare of the children or the fact that, for example, a contact order is not being adhered to, then the court may be prepared to reconsider its decision.

### Financial arrangements

The aim of the new Child Support Act and its administrative arm, the Child Support Agency (CSA), is to standardise the basis on which child maintenance is calculated and paid.

The Act establishes the principle that both parents, whether or not they were ever married, have a duty to contribute to the maintenance of their child. While the courts retain responsibility for related issues such as residence and contact orders, paternity disputes and property orders, the CSA will eventually take control of all financial matters.

The CSA will now take into account some 'clean break' settlements made before April 1993, and in exceptional cases those which came into effect after that date. However, any reduced liability to pay CSA-assessed maintenance in these circumstances will still be calculated according to a strict formula.

The Act also introduces some new terms. A parent who does not live with their own child and where the child is being looked after by someone else is known as an 'absent parent', increasingly referred to colloquially as the liable parent or non-residential parent. The parent or person with whom the child lives and who cares for them on a day-to-day basis is referred to as the 'parent or person with care'. In this situation, where either one or both parents are absent, the child is called a 'qualifying child'.

To find out more about the Child Support Act you can call the CSA on 01345 133133, Monday to Friday 9am to 5pm; calls are charged at local rates. They will also send you an application form for CSA-assessed maintenance and an introductory guide. If you'd like to know about the Act and the CSA in greater detail, the Child Poverty Action Group (CPAG) produces a fairly intelligible guide called the *Child Support Handbook*.

The CSA may charge you for assessing maintenance – and collecting it – if required. However, from April 1995 charges have been suspended for two years and will not apply to applications made after this time. Always check your assessment form to ensure it is correct. In the first year over 50 per cent of all assessments were incorrect and it is expected that only 75 per cent will be correct in year two.

### The CSA timetable

The Act was due to be phased in over a four-year period from April 1993 until April 1997. However, the phase-in period now appears to be open ended.

The courts are no longer able to make assessments for periodical payments for child maintenance where an assessment could be made by the CSA. Court assessments made prior to 1993 can still be varied by the court, although eventually they will come under the CSA's jurisdiction. Essentially, if you can agree between yourselves about financial arrangements for your children then you do not need to use the CSA.

However, if the parent with care applies for, or is in receipt of, a main benefit – Income Support, Family Credit or Disability Working Allowance – the CSA will intervene regardless of any previous maintenance arrangements. The claimant will be asked to complete a maintenance application form.

### Co-operating with the CSA

If you are claiming a benefit such as Income Support you are required to co-operate with the CSA and give them as much information as possible about the absent parent. Failure to do so may result in a loss of benefit.

However, you do not have to supply that information if you think that by doing so you will put yourself or your child at risk or cause undue distress: for example, because the absent parent has a history of violence and you do not want any contact with them. The CSA says that in many cases you will not have to provide evidence of the harm you think will be caused and that your statement will be believed 'unless it is improbable or self-contradictory'.

In addition, if you are now living with a new partner you will also need to provide information about them and also any stepchildren who live with you. For more information see below.

### Child support calculations

Under the new rules, child maintenance calculations have become seriously complex. They are also extremely rigid. The formula is based on current Income Support rates. Below are the general principles of the calculation. If you want to attempt to do your own financial sums, then refer to CPAG's *Child Support Handbook*.

There are five stages to the child support calculation. This formula will not be used to assess absent parents on Income Support, as they will normally have a set amount deducted from their benefit:

### *Stage One: The maintenance requirement*

These are amounts set down by the government to cover the day-to-day expenses of the qualifying child. The maintenance requirement is not an indicator of the minimum or maximum amount of the overall maintenance which is payable.

### *Stage Two: Exempt income*

Exempt income is the level of income an absent parent is allowed to keep before they become liable to pay child maintenance. Exempt income includes allowances for any of the parent's own children who live with them, and in addition allowances for housing costs associated with maintaining a new partner or any stepchildren. Exempt income also applies to the parent with care, since they too are liable to maintain their children. There are proposals to intro-duce a new 'departure system'. This means that in exceptional cases parents can apply to have their case treated individually. Again, there will be strict criteria about who can apply. However, one situa-tion will be where an absent parent has exceptional costs for caring for stepchildren. It is thought that this might arise where, for exam-ple, the natural father is dead and there is no one else to support the child other than the stepfather.

### Stage Three: Assessable income

This is the amount of income that is available to pay child maintenance. Basically it will be the amount you have left once you have deducted your exempt income plus other allowances such as tax and national insurance from your salary, plus half of any occupa-tional pension scheme contributions.

If the total amount of your assessable income exceeds that needed to meet the maintenance requirement, you may have to pay an additional amount of maintenance. Again, this is worked out according to a formula and there is an upper limit on the sum that can be paid.

If either the parent with care or the absent parent lives with a new partner, then the latter's income will be completely disregarded unless they have a joint child. In that case, if the new partner's income exceeds a certain level they will be expected to contribute towards the financial support of their joint child. The allowances for the joint child may be halved when calculating the parent's exempt income and this may have an effect on the overall calculation. This will obviously affect those stepfamilies where one parent is claiming for – or paying maintenance to – the child of a former partner and in addition has a child with their current live-in partner.

### Stage Four: Proposed maintenance

This represents the amount of child maintenance the absent parent is expected to pay, provided that it does not bring their income below the protected income level (see Stage Five). The important principle is that the absent parent pays 50% of their assessable income in child maintenance up to the point where they reach the maintenance requirement figure (see Stage One). After that they contribute at a lower percentage of their income – between 15 and 25% depending on the number of children involved. There is an upper limit to the amount of child maintenance payable under the CSA formula. However, additional maintenance may be claimed through the courts (see next page).

### Stage Five: Protected income

The aim of this is to ensure that the absent parent's disposable income does not fall below a certain level as a result of paying the proposed maintenance. At this stage of the calculation the whole family's expenses and income are taken into account, including those relating to a new partner and stepchildren. With a few exceptions every absent parent will have to pay some child maintenance, even if their level of income falls below the protected minimum.

### Collection and enforcement of payments

The CSA offers a collection service. In most cases the method and timing of the payments will be agreed between the parties. It is also possible to collect payments via the absent parent's employer through a Deduction of Earnings Order. Very simply the maintenance assessment is deducted at source from the absent parent's wages.

The CSA will also chase up any overdue or unpaid maintenance. The Agency can take enforcement action through the courts, but will only do so if it thinks the case merits it and there is a chance of success.

### Reviews and rights of appeal

The CSA carries out three kinds of reviews:

- a regular yearly review,
- reviews to cover changes in circumstances,
- reviews of decisions of the Child Support Officers (CSO).

If you think that a CSO has wrongly assessed your case then you can ask for it to be reviewed. However, you must bear in mind that, for the moment at least, you can only ask for your case to be reconsidered on a technicality – for example, because you think the sums are wrong or the proper procedures have not been adhered to. You won't be entitled to a review just because you think the assessment is 'unfair'.

If your application for a review is refused or you don't believe that the decision made by a CSO following a review is correct, then you can appeal to a Child Support Appeal Tribunal (CSAT). In the case of a refusal to give details of the absent parent you can go straight to the CSAT without needing to apply first for a review. If having received the decision of the CSAT you still feel aggrieved, you can appeal to a Child Support Commissioner on a point of law.

At this stage, you would probably be wise to seek legal advice.

### Shared care

Provided that the child spends at least two nights per week with each parent, then the maintenance calculation will be assessed on a pro rata basis. The proportion of nights the child spends with each person will be averaged out over a year. The parent who looks after the child for the longer period will be regarded as the parent with care, the other parent will be referred to as the absent parent.

If the child is cared for jointly by one parent and another person, then the maintenance payable by the absent parent will be calculated in the usual way. Shared care will not be calculated for anyone who looks after a child for less than two nights a week on average.

### Multiple families

If the absent parent has a number of children by different partners, then the maintenance the absent parent will have to pay will be shared between the parents with care based on their comparative maintenance requirements.

### Additional maintenance

Although the CSA will take over almost all matters relating to child maintenance, the court will still deal with certain specific cases. These include:

- additional child maintenance above the amount that can be awarded under the CSA formula,
- maintenance for stepchildren. Absent parents can be asked to contribute to the maintenance of children who are not their birth or adoptive children but who used to live with the absent parent and who regarded them as members of their family,
- child maintenance to meet the expenses of school or vocational or professional training,
- maintenance to meet the special needs of a child with a disability,
- maintenance from a parent who does not usually live in the UK.

Applications for this type of maintenance should be made in the first place to the Family Proceedings Court in a Magistrates Court.

# PART THREE

## THE FINANCIAL ESSENTIALS

This part of the book looks at the major financial issues like managing your money, investing for your family's future security and handling financial problems. Much of the information applies to everyone, regardless of their family circumstances. However, stepfamilies often find themselves in a particularly pressured and precarious financial situation and therefore it is especially important to be well informed and well prepared.

---

*"Every one of the children make different financial demands but my stepchild attempted to use emotional blackmail – it didn't work."*

---

The following chapters explain the basic principles behind many of the financial schemes that are currently in operation. You will see that at the end of many of the chapters there is a Step Watch section designed to highlight points of interest or concern to stepfamilies.

It is highly unlikely that there will ever be a series of schemes designed to meet the specific needs of stepfamilies. What matters is that as a stepfamily you tailor what is presently available to meet your individual circumstances. Remember too that no two stepfamilies are absolutely alike and therefore the financial demands and constraints will vary from unit to unit.

Bear in mind that the information is very general and that new schemes and legislative changes happen all the time. You should always get independent advice (see page 166) when making any kind of financial planning or trying to solve a cashflow difficulty.

### The big jigsaw

With an ever-burgeoning and increasingly complex personal finance market, it's easy to feel like taking cover in a shoebox under the bed. By ignoring the jargon and following some simple principles you can avoid tripping up in the money minefield. Here are the top seven tips:

1. Go for the big picture. See your financial planning as creating one big jigsaw rather than a series of inconsequential puzzles. Don't forget to take a panoramic view of the financial threads that bind your extended family.

2. Be your own flexible friend and always ask 'what if?' Life has a nasty habit of throwing up the unexpected, especially for step-families, so don't tie up your personal treasury in unbreakable knots.

3. Never sign up for any scheme, whether investing or borrowing, without ensuring you understand exactly how it works and knowing the best and the worst that can happen.

4. Give yourself a tax break. The taxman – or woman – is bound to have a finger in your financial pie. It doesn't take much planning to slim down the size of the Revenue's slice.

5. Review your finances thoroughly at least once a year and certainly whenever your circumstances change.

6. Unless your heart and your bank balance can take the strain, play safe. Leave the high stakes to the pages of a John Gresham thriller.

7. Always take independent advice. Avoid the sales pitch and go for the consulting room. (For more information see page 166.)

---

*"I felt alarmed when my eldest stepson asked us for money to buy a property. He hasn't followed this up yet but I realise I have to guard against unfairness and not being even handed. We gave our youngest stepson a loan to purchase a house but he has a very different way of approaching us for money, he's far less pushy."*

---

## MANAGING YOUR MONEY

In a consumer-led society where 'spend' is the war cry, it isn't difficult to live beyond your means. Money represents different things to different people. As you will probably have realised from the exercises in Part One, money can confer power, status and control. Yet in itself it can also be a controlling device.

It doesn't matter whether you're a millionaire with money slushing around Swiss vaults or you're desperately keeping your account from turning a darker shade of pink, either way you'll lose out if you don't keep your cashflow in check.

Thorough budgeting is the key to managing your finances properly, especially in a stepfamily. If you don't know what comes into your piggy bank, where it goes when it leaves and what it does while it's waiting to be spent, then you're going to have a tough time making any kind of sensible financial decisions.

Setting and keeping to a budget stops nasty surprises like bouncing cheques; getting your son a second pair of football boots while your stepdaughter goes without a birthday gift; spending a miserable day on a windy British seaside prom when you could be sunning yourself in the Med.

The aim of drawing up a budget is to:

- establish exactly how much income you have coming in, from whatever source,
- set out all your expenditure,
- enable you to spot ways you might maximise your income,
- prioritise your financial responsibilities (see page 46),
- plan for the future.

## Your personal financial audit

If you have a perfectly totted-up and recorded personal budget to hand, then skip this section. If not, read on. Making your first ever proper budget, or reworking your finances when your circumstances change, can be an arduous task. However, once it's done, regular updating and reviewing will make the whole process far simpler. Scratchings on the backs of envelopes and other debris do not count as proper budgets.

If you have access to a computer then there are lots of personal accounting packages around which can be a big help. You may need to invest a little time initially to get the program to work effectively for you, but in the long run budgeting and tax calculations are so much easier.

It's best if you run this personal financial audit through your entire family unit – including children if they have any savings. The checklist opposite has been formulated for one person, so don't forget that most of your expenditure like Council Tax, household bills and so on will be duplicated if you put them down on each person's audit.

Before you start you should gather together the following essential ingredients: wage slips or pay packets; tax advice and other correspondence; benefit books; savings books; investment and savings certificates; maintenance agreements and any other financial agreements; details of loans including any mortgage; utility bills; credit card statements; demands for unpaid bills; court judgments; and any other piece of paper that records or reflects your income and expenditure.

You will also need a fresh pad of paper, pencil and eraser or computer program. Finally, find yourself somewhere quiet where you won't be disturbed until the deed is done. Go through the checklist on page 93.

**WATCH OUT!**

**Watch out!** Decide in advance whether you're going to work out your budget on an annual, monthly or weekly basis, and then ensure that every calculation is done to that scale.

## The bigger picture

In addition to working out your average weekly or monthly expenditure, you should also put down on paper all your capital savings. It's sensible to break them into three lists: Untouchables – savings like pensions that you can't get your hands on; Possibles – savings that will mature in the next year or so, or savings that you could realistically cash in if you had to; and Now Money – accessible savings.

Against this you should set any special major outgoings in the foreseeable future. These might include: a new baby; child or stepchild's wedding; buying a car; divorce; legal costs; moving house, and so on.

# INCOME

| Work | £ |
|------|---|
| Full-time work | |
| Part-time work | |
| Commission | |
| Any additional earnings | |

**Maintenance**
Yourself
Your children

**State benefits**
(list each one and how much)

**Investment Income**
(list each source and how much)

**Other Income**

# EXPENDITURE

| Tax | £ | Household bills | £ |
|-----|---|----------------|---|
| Income tax (if not already deducted) | | Water | |
| National insurance (if self employed) | | Gas | |
| | | Electricity | |
| **Maintenance** | | Telephone | |
| Your former partner(s) | | TV | |
| Your children | | Cable | |
| Other contributions to former partner(s) and family | | Food | |
| | | General goods | |
| **Work** | | **Car** | |
| Travelling | | Tax | |
| Lunch | | Petrol | |
| Other work | | Service | |
| **Your home** | | **School** | |
| Mortgage (including mortgage protection plan and other associated costs) | | Fees | |
| | | Uniforms | |
| Rent | | Other activities | |
| Ground rent | | **Childcare** | |
| Council tax | | Nanny/childminder | |
| | | Baby-sitting | |
| **Insurance** | | **Eldercare** | |
| House | | Residential care | |
| Contents | | Home helps | |
| Car | | Visiting | |
| Life | | **Personal spending** | |
| Private medical insurance | | Clothes | |
| Permanent health cover | | Cosmetics | |
| Other insurance | | Sport/personal fitness | |
| **Pensions** (List each one) | | Hobbies | |
| | | Subscriptions | |
| **Savings plans** (List each one and include regular amounts you put away for things like holidays) | | Entertainment | |
| | | Holidays (don't duplicate this if it's covered under 'Savings plans') | |
| **Outstanding debts** | | Transport (other than car) | |
| Loans | | Charities | |
| HP agreements | | Other expenditure | |
| Credit card bills | | | |
| Utilities | | | |
| Other debts | | | |

**Total Income £**

**Total Expenditure £**

*"My partner is expecting me to pay all my daughter's wedding bills from a small legacy I received. It's not really a problem, just a small niggle."*

## Making sense of your budget

Making endless lists of income and expenditure is the first step. Once you've done this, you must review your financial situation. It doesn't matter whether you're in the black and your calculations show a healthy 'profit', or you're deeply in the red and there's a yawning gap between what's coming in and what's going out. You always need to ask yourself: How can I manage my money more efficiently?

Here's a quick round up of the things you ought to be thinking about:

### In the black?

- <u>Income exceeding expenditure</u>: look at ways to increase your savings. Never leave large amounts of cash in regular bank current accounts – earn money on it. Perhaps you can afford to re-assess your lifestyle, pay off your mortgage or improve your home.

- <u>High borrowings but healthy, easy-access savings</u>: use some of your savings to pay off your debts. Remember that you'll pay out far more borrowing money that you'll earn in interest on your savings.

For more information about investment opportunities see page 100.

### In the red?

- <u>Expenditure exceeding income</u>: you'll need to think about two things, ways to maximise your income and ways to cut down on your expenditure. This is often much easier to talk about than actually to put into practice. Below you will find some budget-efficient ideas.

## Can you improve your cashflow?

There's no quick and easy way to getting out of a tight financial corner, but here are some suggestions that might help ease your cash crisis.

- If you pay or receive maintenance and you find yourself in financial difficulty, always investigate revising your maintenance arrangements.

- If your earnings are low or you rely on benefits, make sure that you are receiving everything you are entitled to (see page 131), but see Watch out! on page 96.

- If you're a lazy late payer, use direct debits to pay your key bills. Always keep an eye on your bank statements to make sure your account has been correctly debited.

- If you find it difficult to budget, investigate the pre-payment facilities offered by the gas and electricity companies.

- Go through bank and other statements with a keen eye – mistakes can often crop up and go undetected. It always pays to check thoroughly.

- Make sure your tax rating is correct. If you're a non-tax-payer ensure that interest on your savings is paid without tax deducted (see page 155).

- If your telephone bills are bringing you down, consider using the phone for incoming calls only. You could think about installing a coin meter for phone-happy teenagers. Mercury or cable might prove cheaper, especially if you make long-distance calls. It is also possible to put a bar on certain numbers being dialled – contact your phone provider for more details.

- Bulk shopping can save money but go with a list and keep to it – it's easy to overspend when everything looks like a cheap buy.

- Consider asking adult non-dependants for a realistic contribution towards their bed and board. This can be a really difficult one, because often parental responsibility evokes a sense of guilt at asking offspring to pay a commercial rate – or something approaching it. In addition, you may already have agreed other trade-offs like childcare or feel that the family should stick together in financial difficulty.

- If you have a car, consider whether you really need to run it. Car owning can take a considerable amount of your income. If things are tight and you need four wheels, then you may want to trade down to keep the insurance low.

- Avoid penny-pinching gains with serious pound consequences, like dropping your household insurance – you could end up losing everything.

A word of caution. If you're on a very low income, then be realistic, it's difficult to budget effectively. Many ways of increasing the free cash you have around may be hard to achieve. For example, a lot of people on low incomes don't shop in large supermarkets where prices tend to be lower. Reasons for this range from the temptation to overspend to a lack of private transport to out-of-town sites. If you don't have much money, then you are likely to buy inferior goods. Although they do for the time being they don't last as long and need replacing. If you're on benefits then your budgeting will essentially be an attempt at checks and balances. Opportunities to maximise your income may well affect your benefit levels and ultimately leave you worse off.

## Your account or mine?

The big dilemma for many couples is how to divide up their bank and savings accounts – whether to keep their financial affairs as separate as they can or pool all their resources into one big family pot. Increasingly many people are becoming more protective of their own money and less willing to commit their capital and their earnings to the big pot. There are number of good reasons for this:

1. Cohabiting couples ought to be wary about joint accounts for the reasons outlined on page 78. Unless your individual income and expenditure is exactly the same, you may end up out of pocket if the relationship turns sour.

2. If you've already had your fingers burnt in one financially dubious relationship you may be less than willing to let your new partner dip into 'your' money – however honest or trustworthy they actually are.

---

*"I am much more in control of my and the family's finances. In my previous relationship my partner gave me no control at all. I've had to work to achieve this."*

---

3. You may bring into the relationship certain key financial responsibilities like children or a home. In these circumstances you could be unwilling to risk anything that might undermine your responsibility to meet your financial obligations.

> *"I have felt resentful in the past about Ron buying too many presents and quite expensive ones for his son when we were struggling to move house."*

4. You might enter a new relationship in a stronger financial position, for example because you've improved your employment prospects or benefited from a divorce settlement or an inheritance. In your previous partnerships you may have felt financially vulnerable and may now be unwilling to surrender any of your new-found financial strength.

> *"In my previous marriage my partner was absolutely against me earning my own income. I handled the finances but we struggled when the children were young. Now my second husband and I have to earn enough for ourselves plus our four children. Now I feel I have the freedom to choose, I enjoy earning my own living."*

5. Independence is critical for many people. It's good to feel that you are in control of your financial well-being and that you can meet your day-to-day needs without having to ask someone else for money.

> *"It was my decision not to have a joint bank account. My ex-husband drained our joint account without me realising. I felt more in control in this marriage by having my own account and managing my own finances. I wish I had not felt the need to retain financial independence."*

Remember, if you are married the notion of 'his' or 'her' accounts is more or less irrelevant. If you split up all your money, from whatever source, can be pooled if the court is called on to make a settlement.

Having said that, it's worth considering the pros and cons of a variety of single and joint account options.

**Two singles**

*Pros*

- Separate accounts let you each control your own financial destiny. This is particularly good if you have different attitudes towards money and different spending habits.

> *"I keep my personal finances separate from my husband.*
> *He gives me a housekeeping allowance but this is a source of*
> *tension. I have to manage on too small an allowance and make*
> *up the difference with my own private money.*
> *My first husband and I discussed money freely but we don't*
> *discuss financial matters at all."*

*Cons*

- This arrangement can work very well when both of you are earning similar incomes. It's unlikely to continue to be viable if one of you stops working or takes a severe cut in salary.
- You need to be very disciplined about meeting your major household expenditure. Standing orders from one account or the other may help. If either or both of you are slap-dash about managing your money, this arrangement could well fall flat on its face.

> *"We decided to keep everything very separate and trust each*
> *other to pay up jointly for whatever we need. More importantly*
> *not to criticise the other for long phone calls, expensive cars or*
> *clothes if we can afford to pay for them!"*

- To some extent, solo accounts tend to emphasise the notion of two individuals rather than a single partnership. It's easier to fall into the,'I paid for, you paid for' argument and move away from the concept of joint financial responsibility.

> *"We each have a current account. My partner pays*
> *the household expenses, I buy food and pay for domestic help.*
> *Redecorating and holidays are paid for jointly.*
> *I would prefer to have a joint account but my partner*
> *doesn't want one."*

## One joint account

### Pros

- Pooling all your money into one account is by far the easiest way to ensure that you pay all your household and other bills. You stop the messy business of transferring money from one account to another or suddenly finding that you've incurred bank charges because there are insufficient funds in your account.

### Cons

- You don't have any financial privacy. This may mean that you could resent your partner taking money out of the account to buy something personal and possibly 'extravagant'. Equally, one person might feel reticent about withdrawing money to purchase an item for themselves which they consider a luxury.

---

*"I've had to practise spending money on me – a hangover from single parent days when everything was from jumble sales and last minute shopping for reduced food stuffs."*

---

- Problems can also arise if one partner is not working or earning very much and therefore not contributing to the joint account. In these circumstances they may not feel 'entitled' to take money out for their personal use.

## One joint, two singles

### Pros

- Possibly the best compromise. This allows you to have a joint account for all your household bills as well as enabling each of you to maintain your financial independence though your personal accounts.

---

*"We both maintain separate bank accounts plus a joint one to which we both contribute equal amounts. That pays for the major household expenditure. We don't want to discuss everything to do with money, only those things which affect the household."*

---

- To make this work you'll need a standing order from each of your accounts to the joint one. Watch out that you align the movement of money so that, for example, your salary enters your account before the standing order leaves it and that money then arrives before your mortgage is debited from the joint account.

*Cons*

- Avoid developing fancy schemes to shift money around numerous accounts. Unless you're extremely smart – and also a money expert – you'll probably end up incurring unnecessary bank charges as you miss your debiting deadlines.

## MONEY IN: INVESTING

Whether you put away the odd couple of pounds for a summer sunshine break or you win the lottery and are contemplating early retirement, remember that money can make money. The investment game is all about getting your hard-won cash to work for you. You don't need to be a millionaire to play the game, the smallest savings can still yield some extra pounds.

Most of the savings and investment schemes around are simply a sophisticated version of the traditional piggy bank, only these days they're likely to bring home a bit more bacon. If you want to put your pennies to work you have four broad options:

- a savings account,
- the stock market,
- property,
- a pension or insurance-linked scheme.

However you choose to invest your money, spread the load and don't put all your eggs in one basket. Unless you have very special personal circumstances, you'd probably be best off selecting a series of products in each of these categories.

## Before you invest

If you've given yourself a thorough personal financial audit (see page 93) then you'll have a fair idea of your range of commitments and future needs. To concentrate your mind further on making investments you'll need to think about the following:

- Your age. Not only will you have different financial priorities at different stages in your life, but your ability to invest and make returns will also be constrained by age. In terms of a pension, for example, the 10 years between your twenties and thirties might not seem like a long time in the general scheme of things, but in investment terms waiting that extra decade to begin to make provision for your retirement could cost you dear.

- Your family commitments. For stepfamilies, this is perhaps the biggest moveable feast. You have to focus on two key priorities. First flexibility, so that you have room to manoeuvre if your circumstances change – and they probably will. Second, how you will survive in older age. This is particularly important for women whose earning capacity and ability to provide for an adequate pension might be limited by carer responsibilities.

- Your health. Any known health problems might mean that you'll have difficulties getting decent life assurance cover. Therefore, you may need to look at other ways of accruing capital, especially if bad health could prevent you from working.

- Future expectations. Although you don't want to count your chickens before they've hatched, it's still important to look ahead. For example, is your salary likely to continue to rise or, apart from inflation increases, have you reached the peak of your earning power? Is there a chance that you might inherit some money or property? Will you have additional income to cushion the risks of higher return investments?

- Your tax position. Whether you're a non-tax-payer (you earn less than your current tax allowance) or you pay at the basic or higher rate of tax will make a difference to the investments you should make. Schemes providing special tax breaks offer no benefits to non-tax-payers, while higher-rate payers may be able to reduce their tax liability by careful investments.

### Narrowing the choice

To a certain extent the amount of savings you have available will dictate the kind of schemes you can invest in. Many schemes stipulate a minimum first investment and there's often a ceiling on the maximum you can put in. Some accounts are designed for small savers, for others you'll need a couple of thousand pounds before it's worth investing. To help yourself and your adviser narrow the field you also need to ask yourself these five questions:

1. Am I investing for a regular income right now or am I saving for the long term? Many schemes do not exclude one route or the other and allow you to do a bit of both.

2. How much of a risk can I afford to take? The more you stand to gain through your investment, the more you risk losing. Only play the higher stakes when you are sure you've met your day-to-day needs – and that includes having enough to live on when the wrinkles appear. If you're a natural worrier, play safe and enjoy what you get.

3. Will I want access to my money in the near future? The higher the return the longer you'll probably need to shut your money away for. If you want instant access, check you can get it. Remember, many schemes penalise you for withdrawing money earlier than specified.

4. Will the scheme do what I want it to do? Some schemes are tied into particular savings needs, for example school fees. Think carefully before you lock yourself in to a scheme that limits your spending choices.

5. Will the savings scheme or investment keep up with inflation? Inflation means that money loses its value. In ten years' time £5 will buy you considerably less than it does today. Promises of large returns do not necessarily equal an effective investment in real terms after you take inflation into account.

## Savings accounts

Most simple savings accounts are to be found either through high street banks and building societies, the Post Office or through other government schemes. In fact, because the traditional high street accounts are so common and so secure many people don't even think of them as serious financial investments. However, they can play an important role in your overall financial planning. Here are some of the schemes you'll come across:

### Instant access and notice accounts

The banks and building societies offer a range of basic savings accounts. Some of these allow you to withdraw your money immediately, for others you have to give a specified period of notice which can be anything from seven days to six months.

Many building societies offer postal accounts which give better returns than branch-based accounts. The minimum initial investment is higher. However, they may be useful if you live a long way from your nearest building society.

Usually the longer you're required to leave your money in before you can withdraw it and the larger the amount of your investment, the greater the rate of interest. Some accounts have tiered rates. Most will give a variable rate of interest, so keep an eye open for what's on offer.

It's worth reviewing your accounts regularly – the best deal six months ago may not be the finest on offer today. However, don't chop and change for the sake of it. To a certain extent it's swings and roundabouts and usually not worth incurring penalties just to chase the highest interest rates.

Interest gained on bank and building society accounts is subject to tax. This is deducted at the basic rate at source – in other words, before you get to take the money out of your account. If you're a non-tax-payer – including children – ask to sign the special declaration form. This means that any interest you earn will be paid to you gross – without tax deducted. It's important to do this, since claiming a tax refund at a later stage could take time and you may as well benefit from the extra cash. Higher-rate tax payers will be liable to pay additional tax on the difference between the basic and higher rates of tax.

### TESSAs (Tax Exempt Special Savings Schemes)

These are a wise option for tax payers over 18 as the account earns you tax-free interest provided that you don't touch your original investment for five years. You can only have one TESSA at a time and there's a cap on the total amount you can invest each year. Although you can swap your TESSA from one bank or building society to another, you may pay a penalty for the privilege of doing so. You may also lose out on a possible loyalty bonus for sticking with the same institution for the whole five years.

## Budget accounts

If your cashflow is tight then a budget account might help you balance the books. Basically you pay in a specified sum of money each month and you can then borrow up to a certain multiple of that amount. If you remain in credit you'll earn interest, if you borrow the extra money then you'll have to pay interest on it. Check the interest charged on loans.

## Credit cards

Although not strictly a savings account, judicious use of a credit card can help you manage your month-to-month budget. Provided that you settle up dead on time and don't use the card as an extra overdraft, it can make sense to use your card. Your savings can then keep earning you interest in a deposit account until you have to pay off the month's credit card spending.

## Government savings schemes

To help it fund its borrowing programme, the government has set up a number of mostly very low-risk savings schemes for members of the public.

## National Savings

There are a variety of schemes available through the Post Office which can be attractive to both tax payers and non-tax-payers. National Savings interest rates don't fluctuate as often as those on bank and building society accounts; while this might be an advantage when interest rates are tumbling, the returns may not be so good if rates rise rapidly. On the whole, in order to reap the maximum benefit from schemes such as tax-free National Savings Certificates you'll need to hang on to the investment for the full term, which is usually five years.

Investing over your local Post Office counter might seem a cosy thing to do, but check whether the rates are competitive for your needs. At the same time, don't dismiss the schemes either.

## Premium bonds

Basically, premium bonds are a state-sponsored lottery without the hype. In investment terms, they are a complete non-starter – if you trade them in you'll get back exactly what you paid, except that in real terms it won't be worth as much. However, if you want a flutter without losing your bet altogether, have a go. After all, the winnings are tax free.

## Investing through the stock market

There are two main types of investment quoted on the stock market – equities and fixed interest stocks. To put it simply, equity means a company's capital – its assets, profits and so on. A share is a slice of that capital and therefore for each share you own, you own a proportion of the company. In recognition of this you normally receive an income or dividend from the company. Each share can be sold – and resold – and its value will depend on the state of the market and how well the company is doing.

Fixed interest stocks, or securities, give you a guaranteed income which is set in advance. These can be issued by companies or by the government, in which case they are known as gilts. So long as you buy them when they are first issued and leave your investment alone for the specified term, they offer a rock-solid way of providing a guaranteed return over a fixed period. However, if you sell them before they mature or you buy them some time after they are first issued, then you risk the vagaries of the stock market. Gilts can be purchased through the Post Office.

Investing in stocks and shares is far more risky than stashing away your cash in a bank or building society, but then again the rewards could be much greater. However, for the average domestic investor it doesn't have to be high drama and shirt off your back time. It's not difficult to play relatively safe.

There are two ways to invest in stocks and shares: directly by buying shares yourself or through a Personal Equity Plan (PEP); or indirectly together with lots of other people through collective schemes such as unit trusts and investment trusts.

### Buying shares directly

When you buy shares you become part owner of a company and the success of your investment will mirror the profitability of the company as well as the general economic climate. Although there are many types of shares, the most common are ordinary shares. These give you a dividend – a share of the business's profits – and usually a vote at the shareholders' meeting.

Enough amateur investors got their fingers burnt buying stocks and shares in the late 1980s to learn that this is a risky business. Unless you've got serious amounts of money and can pay a broker to buy and sell for you, you'll have to be very dedicated to play the stock market. You must know what you're up to and have money to burn, or else don't risk your life savings. There are however, other ways to go about reaping the potential rewards of the stock market.

## Personal Equity Plans (PEPs)

This is an altogether different – and tax-efficient – stocks and shares investment opportunity. Although it's not a scheme for those looking for a quick profit, it does enable you to put money into the stock market while getting tax relief on your returns. Any dividends or gains when you sell your shares are tax free. Not surprisingly, there's a limit on the amount of money you can invest each year and you can only have one PEP at a time.

It's up to you to choose whether you decide on the investments yourself or leave the decision to a fund manager. It is possible to invest, to a limited extent, in unit trusts or investment trusts through a PEP.

People frequently buy PEPs because they want the tax relief. However, what really matters is that you first choose the kind of investment you want to make and then choose the means by which to make it. For this reason, PEPs may not be ideal for everyone.

## Buying indirectly through unit and investment trusts

Both unit and investment trusts work by individual investors pooling their resources to buy shares in a range of companies. The way the pooled fund is invested is determined by the fund manager, usually a major financial institution. The fund manager will charge a fee for their services which will be taken out of the fund itself. Both unit and investment trusts offer a way of investing in shares by spreading the risks involved.

It's up to the professional fund manager to decide how your money is invested. Unlike buying shares yourself, you won't have a direct say. However, you can choose a unit or investment trust that will only invest in certain types of company. Ethical funds, for example, won't buy into tobacco or weapons companies.

Your main consideration is to choose an investment manager. Your financial adviser will help you do this. You should always check the manager's investment record – although past performance is no guarantee as to how well they'll do in the future.

Although these kind of investments are usually only effective in reward terms in the long run, they do offer flexibility. Many will allow you to contribute regular monthly amounts rather than have to put down a large lump sum. If you get into difficulties you can stop contributing for a while, and if things get really tough, you can always sell off your investment without incurring any penalties.

There are technical differences between unit and investment trusts but these should not make any material difference to the small investor. During 1995 investment managers will also be introducing Open Ended Investment Companies (OEICs) which will operate in a similar way to unit trusts.

## Investing in property

For many people their home is their single biggest investment. Some people go one step further and invest in a second property, either as a holiday home or to rent out. If you're planning to buy a property solely for investment purposes – as opposed to somewhere for you and your family to live – then you need to think about the time and money it will take to manage and maintain it.

You can use your own home as an investment, by for example buying a larger property than you actually need and then selling it on retirement, buying somewhere smaller and investing the difference. Alternatively you could consider paying off your mortgage. In recent years returns for property owners have been poor and the work involved can make this an unattractive investment opportunity.

## Insurance-linked savings plans and pensions

### Insurance-linked savings plans

Most people think of insurance policies in terms of straight forward 'just-in-case' protection against theft or accidents or ill health. In fact, many life insurance policies do more than simply protect your family from the worst, they can also help you save a useful nest egg.

Protection only policies that only pay out if you die during the life of the policy are known as term assurance. These are explained more fully on page 115. This kind of policy tends to be very cheap and the benefits are obviously limited. In contrast, endowment policies which provide an investment opportunity could also pay out a handsome dividend if you survive until the policy matures, although they are more expensive. It is possible to pay one-off, rather than regular amounts into insurance-linked savings schemes.

In investment terms, it's worth thinking about insurance policies not only to protect your nearest and dearest but also as a key part in your personal finance jigsaw. Remember though that these are designed as long-term savings plans and if you cash in your policy early you may not get all your money back.

### Whose life can you insure?

Subject to certain age and health restrictions, almost anyone can insure their own life. Providing you can prove you have an insurable interest in it, you can also insure someone else's life. However, to do this, you will have to prove that you would suffer some kind of financial loss if they were to die. Increasing numbers of fathers are now insuring their non-working wives' lives on the basis that if the latter were to die, the surviving parent would be left with substantial childcare, housekeeping and other costs.

One word of caution for cohabitees. Although husbands and wives are automatically regarded as having an insurable interest in each other's lives, couples living together are not. In practice, for mortgage-linked endowment and similar policies this is not an issue. In other circumstances there are ways round this restriction. For example, you could name your partner as a beneficiary of a policy you take out on your life, or else you could take out a policy in your own name and assign the benefit of it to your partner in your will. If you are in this situation you would be wise to seek professional advice about what to do.

### With-profits endowment policies

These are long-term savings plans where you make a regular contribution to an insurance company normally for at least 10 years. Your contributions, along with the premiums paid by all the other policyholders, are invested in a spread of shares and other investments including property. Every year when the profits of the company are announced bonuses are declared and added to the value of your policy. Once added, the bonuses cannot be taken away. This means that at the end of the term of the policy, you get your money back plus the extra cash you've gained in accumulated bonuses. In addition you may get an extra final bonus. Policies usually guarantee a minimum return, but in practice the bonuses you receive will normally increase your returns beyond that minimum.

### Unit-linked life insurance

Although these schemes work in a similar way to the with-profit endowment policies, they can be more risky – and therefore if you pick the right policy, possibly more profitable. With unit-linked plans the insurance company invests your contributions in units similar to those in a unit trust. Your end-of-term payout will exactly mirror the performance of the investments the company selects.

On all regular payment insurance schemes remember that you'll pay heavy penalties if you cash in your policy early.

## Pensions

Anyone due to retire after the year 2000 who hasn't made adequate provision for their old age needs to do some serious thinking. If you're relying on a State pension to see you through your final decades, you could be in for a fairly impoverished dotage.

The way you approach making financial provision for later life is likely to depend on two things – your age and your working status. Although company and private pension schemes are tax-efficient ways of providing for the future, other savings and investment schemes such as the life assurance plans explained above can also help. Remember, you can only contribute to a pension scheme if you're actually in work. As a non-worker, even if you have the cash, you won't be entitled to enjoy the tax breaks offered by pension schemes and you ought to consider other savings options.

At the moment there are three sources of pensions: the State, employers and private plans. Here is the choice on the pension supermarket shelf.

### The state pension

State pension provision consists of two separate schemes: the basic retirement pension and the State Earnings-Related Pension Scheme (SERPS). The latter is an additional pension which is linked to your full-time or part-time earnings.

Both of these schemes are funded through National Insurance Contributions (NICs). If you're self-employed then you alone are responsible for making the contributions. If you're employed by someone else, then your employer will also pay towards your NICs. You can get a forecast of your potential state pension by completing form BR19 which is available from your local DSS office.

### SERPS

You will automatically pay into SERPS unless you're self-employed and therefore not eligible to belong, or you're employed by someone else and decide to contract out of SERPS.

Contracting out can happen in one of two ways. Your employer may have contracted out because it provides a company pension scheme which offers benefits at least as good as those given by SERPS. Or you can decide to contract out yourself and the government will pay part of your NICs into a personal pension plan of your choice. In addition, the government will currently pay you an incentive bonus for making the transfer.

It's worth noting that the benefits of a SERPS pension have been severely curtailed. For anyone retiring after the year 2000, you'll only receive a SERPS pension of up to a maximum of your average earnings over your lifetime. Under the previous rules you would have got 25% based on your best 20 years' earnings. What's more, if you qualify for your partner's SERPS pension, then after the turn of the next century you'll only be able to inherit half of that pension.

### Company pensions

The advantage of being invited to join a company pension is that your employer contributes to the scheme as well. Company pension schemes operate in one of two ways. First, there is the final salary scheme, which is sometimes called a defined benefit scheme. The second type is a money-purchase scheme, which is also known as a defined contribution scheme.

### *Final salary schemes*

These are the more popular type of company pension plans for large companies. Most schemes require that you make a contribution of about 5% of your earnings, although some are non-contributory. If you do have to make contributions then you won't be taxed on that amount of your earnings.

Final salary schemes guarantee to pay you a proportion of your wages. The best schemes provide up to a maximum of two-thirds of your final salary. Typically pensioners get one-sixtieth of their salary at retirement for each year of employment. If you want to, you have the option of taking a lump sum payment and a smaller pension.

In the event of your reaching retirement age and the pension fund having insufficient money to pay you the promised pension, the employer would usually meet the shortfall.

It's worth checking exactly what your employer has to offer. Some schemes provide extra benefits for your partner and dependants when you die or if you die in service.

### *Money-purchase schemes*

In these schemes your pension benefits are directly related to how much you and your employer contribute and how well that money is invested. Unlike final salary schemes, there's no guaranteed fixed income when you retire and what you get may bear no relation to the salary you were earning. On retirement you'll receive a percentage of the money that's been invested in the form of a lump sum payment. The remainder will be re-invested to buy you a regular pension or annuity from a life assurance company.

### Pension boosters

Although you may be a member of a company pension scheme you may not feel that this is sufficient to enable you to retire in comfort. If you've got the spare cash and you want to increase your retirement income, there are two ways to boost your pension savings.

You can either pay extra money into the company pension scheme through Additional Voluntary Contributions (AVCs), or you can contribute to your own private arrangement called Free Standing Additional Voluntary Contributions (FSAVCs). The latter work on the money-purchase principle and allow you to determine the level of investment risk as well as the range of benefits. However, on retirement the money must be used to purchase a pension. AVCs may work on either the money-purchase or final salary principle. Contributions to both types of scheme attract tax relief.

### Job changers

If you tend to move around the job market the picture isn't as bleak as it used to be as far as occupational pension schemes go. If you change jobs you can do one of three things.

1. Simply leave your existing pension where it is. When you retire you will get a pension from your old employer based on your salary and the contributions you made up until the time you left.

2. Arrange for an amount of money representing your accrued pension entitlement to be invested by an insurance company, rather like a personal pension plan.

3. Transfer your accrued pension entitlement to your new company pension scheme. This way you can 'buy' yourself some extra years.

Ensuring you choose the right option is very complex and you must always seek independent advice.

### Personal pensions

Personal Pension Plans (PPPs) are essentially long-term savings schemes available to any worker who is self-employed or not part of a company pension scheme. The important thing to remember is that this kind of policy can only pay out once you reach at least 50 or if you die before then. Under no circumstances will you be able to get your money out sooner.

Personal pensions are an extremely tax-efficient way of saving and the earlier you start the better – and cheaper. PPPs can also offer you the flexibility of making lump sum payments as well as regular contributions. If you do get into financial deep water you can put your contributions on hold. To a limited extent you can catch up later on when your cash is flowing more easily.

You can elect to take the benefit of a PPP at any time after your fiftieth birthday – you do not need to have stopped work. Up to one-quarter of the money in the scheme can be taken as a cash lump sum. The balance is used to buy you an annuity which provides you with a regular income. You can decide whether you want the income to be paid to you for the rest of your life only, or whether you want a smaller pension to be paid to you and then following your death to continue to be paid to your surviving spouse. If you and your partner are unmarried there can be a problem in ensuring that your partner is entitled to a widow's pension and you must seek expert advice.

The personal pension market is very complex and it's worth taking good advice before you make a decision which could literally affect you to the end of your days.

Like endowment life insurance, PPPs come in two basic varieties – with-profits and unit-linked. Unless you're of a very nervous disposition or you're only a few years off retirement, it's probably worth going for a mix of the two.

### With-profits pension plans

These are set up by life assurance companies who invest your money on your behalf. You are guaranteed a minimum return. In addition, the profits generated by the investments provide you with an annual bonus, which once awarded is then guaranteed and cannot be taken away. Also, at the end of the life of the policy you may also get an additional final bonus.

### Unit-linked pension plans

Like all unit-linked schemes these pension plans can be more risky, but they may also yield some very high rewards. What you get will depend on how well your investments perform. And although they might do extremely well throughout your working life, a series of stock market tumbles just before you retire could drastically reduce your pension entitlement. To avoid this risk, unit-linked schemes have switching facilities. This means that as you approach retirement you can move your investments to a 'deposit fund' or a 'gilt fund' which is invested in low-risk, interest-bearing investments.

## The 'money in' checklist

Here are some questions you might like to go over with your financial adviser, bank or building society.

### On investments

- Will I have instant access and if not how long is the notice period for withdrawals?
- What is the rate of interest and how often is it paid?
- What are the tax advantages to me as a non/basic/higher-rate tax payer?
- Do I have to leave my money in for a set period of time and are there any penalties for withdrawing early?
- What are the minimum and maximum investments I can make?
- Is there a limit on how often I can invest money or on how many of these accounts I can hold?
- What are the risks of this investment?

### On pensions (some will apply only to PPPs)

- What benefits will my dependants be entitled to?
- What happens if I cannot continue making contributions?
- At what age can I retire?
- What happens if I die before I retire?
- Can I make both lump sum and regular contributions?
- What options do I get on retirement?

1. If you decide to move in with a new partner and not get married, then be careful how you deal with your cash. If you pool all your savings and income into one account then the law will regard this as a common purse. In other words, it considers that the money is always intended for both your benefits. Should you split up and take the matter to court, then the judge is likely to split the contents of any joint account equally, regardless of who put what in.

The same will apply to any major investments you make together, so you need to think carefully about what would happen if you split up. Your partner won't be able to touch investments you make in your own name unless you leave the contents to them in your will.

The law also assumes that if you have a joint account, you trust each other. Therefore, if one of you takes money from that account to buy a personal item, say clothing – even if the other partner actually invested the money in the first place – then that item will be regarded as belonging to the person who bought it.

2. Most children will be non-tax-payers (see page 156). Therefore if they have a bank or building society account you should make sure that they complete form R85. This will ensure that any income they receive on their investments is paid without tax having being deducted.

3. As a parent, you cannot use your child's tax-free status to salt away your income from the clutches of the Inland Revenue. Any income produced by an investment which you bought for the child will be considered for tax purposes to be your own. However, if you do put money into your child's savings account, the first £100 of income is not attributed to you.

The other sensible thing to do, especially if you are approaching the £100 mark, is to invest your gifts to the child in tax free investments such as National Savings Certificates. If the child has substantial capital which is in danger of generating income above their personal allowance rate, you should make use of these in any case.

4. Income generated by monetary gifts to the child from other relatives or from investments made out of the child's earnings will not be attributed to you for tax purposes.

# EXTRA PLANNING FOR THE FUTURE

## Life assurance

On page 108 we looked at the various types of investment-linked life assurance plans that are available. While these provide you with a useful savings option, some kind of life assurance policy is critical for anyone with dependants. Straightforward life assurance provides your dependants with a cash sum if you die, and there are other policies which pay out if you become incapable of work. The following paragraphs look at pure life insurance without any investment element.

Don't assume that it's only the family breadwinner who needs to insure their life. Anyone who plays a key role in raising children or caring for elderly or disabled dependants and is responsible for running the home will be very expensive to replace in terms of paid help if they die or become incapacitated. Equally, should they fall seriously ill or suffer an accident, the benefits of a policy could be welcome in paying for nursing or other special care.

**Watch out!** If you have a mortgage you may have some kind of loan-linked endowment policy which will give you enough cash to pay off your outstanding mortgage if you die. However, it may not offer sufficient additional cash to provide adequately for your dependants. Check out the provisions of your policy.

WATCH OUT!

There are a variety of different life assurance schemes available. What you need to ensure is that whatever you select offers you adequate cover and doesn't tie your hands if your family circumstances change.

### Term assurance

The cheapest of all life cover, this will pay out if you die before the policy matures. If you survive, you won't get your money back. The important thing is to take out a policy as young as you can, as the premium rates start climbing very steeply once you head towards 'middle age' and beyond.

### Convertible term assurance

This is very much the same as term assurance, except as its name suggests you can convert the policy to another type of life assurance, principally an endowment policy, at a later date. The advantage of this is that it will ensure that you can always obtain life

cover whatever your state of health. The only rider to this is to make sure that the types of policies that you could convert to are equally competitive – you don't want to find that the other policies the company offers aren't worth converting to. Some policies will allow you to convert to another term assurance or even to another convertible term assurance.

Whichever kind of policy you take out, it's very important to make sure that you don't under-insure yourself. This means that you will either have to over-insure when you're young and the premiums are cheap, or else take out a policy that allows you to increase the cover later on.

### Joint life policies vs single life policies

Joint life policies come in two varieties:

- Joint life, first death pays out when the first partner dies, which can help pay off any outstanding mortgage as well offer other financial support.

- Joint life, second death pays out when the second partner dies. It could play an important part in inheritance tax planning for your surviving dependants, as it could help pay off your inheritance tax liability (see page 126). For example:

*Betty and Louis take out a joint life, second death policy. Louis dies and all his property, including his half share in their home, passes directly to Betty. Since gifts and inheritance between spouses don't attract tax, there's nothing to pay to the Inland Revenue. However, when Betty dies her estate is divided up between their three children. The accumulated wealth is now well beyond the tax-free zone and the children will have to pay tax on their inheritance. It's fortunate then that on Betty's death their life assurance policy pays up and the cash helps their children meet the inheritance tax bill.*

However, with the rising divorce rate, joint life policies may not be such a good idea, especially for younger couples. If you take out a joint life policy and you get divorced you are unlikely to want your ex-partner to benefit from the terms of the plan. Added to this, if you do get divorced you are likely to be some years older than when you first took out a life policy and therefore the cost of the premiums, even on a single life policy, could have increased dramatically. For this reason you should each consider very carefully taking out separate policies on your own lives rather than going jointly. In addition, each of you may be offered different terms by different insurers.

You might be better off taking out separate policies from two insurers rather than a joint policy from one.

# Health cover

While many people take the important step of insuring themselves against early death, far fewer consider covering themselves against the more frequent occurrence of accidents or sickness. There are a number of different types of scheme available. It's important to forget about the fear and hype that goes with marketing them and concentrate on whether they deliver the best deal for you and your family.

It's inevitable that in order to get any kind of permanent health cover you have to be in pretty good shape to start with. Because people are more likely to get sick than to die early, premiums for this kind of cover tend to be more expensive and insurance companies usually insist on rigorous health checks.

### Permanent health insurance

Permanent health insurance (PHI) shouldn't be confused with private medical cover. While the latter will pay out for medical consultations, surgery and hospitalisation costs, PHI provides an income if you become incapacitated and unable to work through illness or disability. It is vital for self-employed people, although it may be expensive depending on your occupation. In general non-workers are not eligible for PHI. However, there are policies available for those who are 'housewives'.

There is usually a deferral period (say six months) before the insurance company will actually pay out. The drawback with this is that if you are ill for only five and a half months, for example, you would receive no money from the policy, although you may have lost income if you are not covered by a company sickness scheme. The cheaper the policy, the longer the deferral period tends to be. 'Housewife' policies have a cap on the amount paid out and some may kick in after three months.

The income from a PHI policy is tax-free for the first year and is normally paid until you return to work or until you reach an agreed cut-off age, such as 60.

### Critical illness or dread disease insurance

This fills the gap left by PHI by paying out a lump sum if you contract certain serious illnesses. To some extent the insurance companies play on people's fear of the big killers – cancer and heart disease. It's up to you to look around your colleagues, your lifestyle and your family history and decide whether it's worth the sometimes sizeable premium.

### Hospital cash plans

These will provide you with a specified sum of money if you have to go into hospital.

### Accident insurance

This kind of policy pays out varying amounts if you are incapacitated due to an accident, the benefit depending on the degree of disability suffered.

### Long-term care insurance

This is a relatively new type of insurance. Its aim is to provide the cash to finance long-term nursing care required as a result of illness or more likely old age. Currently anyone with assets of over £8000, and that effectively means anyone with their own home, will have to meet the total cost of their long-term care if they become infirm.

You need to weigh up whether you would prefer to leave your home to your children or other family members when you die, or face the prospect that you may have to sell it in order to raise the cash to pay to be cared for in a nursing or retirement home. There are, however, proposals to amend current practice and safeguard elderly people's savings properly.

## STEP WATCH

1. Since cohabitees are not automatically deemed to have an insurable interest in each other's lives, if you are not married to your partner you will have to take steps to ensure that your partner benefits from any life insurance policies you hold. (This will not apply to certain types of policy, for example mortgage protection, where you will be considered to have an insurable interest.)

There are a number of ways you can get round the problem of insurable interest and you should take advice before you decide what to do because they may have tax and other long term implications. Broadly here are your options:

a. You could take out a policy on your own life and name your partner as the person entitled to the pay-out when you die. Although this means that the benefit will not become part of your estate on your death and therefore not liable for inheritance tax, you will not be able to alter the agreement if your relationship doesn't work out.

b. You could take out a policy on your life and assign the benefit of the policy to your partner. This means that even though the policy is in your name, it would be up to your partner, in principle though not necessarily in practice, to keep up the premiums. Again you won't be able to alter the agreement. If you start another relationship you may find that since you are that much older, the premiums on a fresh policy will be more expensive.

c. You could take out a policy on your life and stipulate that the benefit is held in trust (for example, for your partner or child). This will give you some flexibility to provide for a variety of future scenarios, and depending on the terms of the trust will not necessarily tie you down to a named person.

d. You could take out a policy on your own life so that the benefit forms part of your estate when you die. By making a will you can then ensure that your partner receives the benefit of the pension or life insurance plan. Although this means that you're free to change the terms of your will and therefore the beneficiary of any life policy, whoever receives the payout may have to forfeit some of the cash for inheritance tax.

Whatever you are thinking of doing you should take expert advice before you commit yourself.

2. If you are married then consider nominating your spouse as your beneficiary. However, given the high divorce rate, it may be safer making the policy part of your estate when you die (see the advice to cohabitees above). If you do this, then unlike cohabitees your surviving spouse won't have to pay any inheritance tax since none is payable on gifts between spouses.

3. If you and your partner split up you should amend your death benefit nominations for your pension and any life insurance policies. Depending on how you have set up your life assurance policies, this may not always be possible (see above).

4. A life insurance policy can be a useful way of providing for an adult child or non dependent stepchild. If on your death you plan to give the lion's share of your estate to your dependent children or to your birth children, but you still want to acknowledge the inheritance of an adult son or daughter or non dependent stepchild, consider taking out a life insurance policy and holding the benefit in trust for them. That way they will have an identifiable claim on your estate.

## School fees

Financial advisers acknowledge that when it comes to paying for education many parents bury their heads in the sand and only pull them out when private schooling is way beyond their financial clutches. On a term-by-term basis, the cost of private education can be prohibitive.

The best advice is to start planning as early as you can – even before you try to start a family. However, having said that, you should see any potential school fees as part of your overall financial planning. Don't get locked into a school-fees-only plan in case you don't actually have children or you find that you don't need to pay for their education. Go for flexibility both in terms of how you make your contributions and how you can use your savings.

If you have doting grandparents or other relatives around, get them to contribute as soon as possible. Remember, stepfamilies may have the advantage of four or more sets of grandparents. If they – or you – can afford to put down a substantial lump sum, then educational trusts offer a tax-free way of making considerable savings on schooling costs.

## STEP WATCH

1. If you have already made provision for your birth children to attend a private school and perhaps benefit from reduced fees, enquire whether any stepchildren will be able to secure the same terms. However, if you've been able to obtain a special rate as a lone parent, then this might be jeopardised if you marry a new partner.

2. If you are applying for maintenance from a former partner remember that the CSA calculation won't take school fees into account. You will need to go through the court to obtain contributions for schooling.

3. A step-parent's income will not be taken into account when making an assessment for a student grant.

## WHERE THERE'S A WILL, THERE'S A WAY

Facing up to the fact that one day you will die is tough, and is the reason that so many people fail to get down to making a will. Yet the big problem is that as personal wealth grows through increases in property values, life assurance policies and the rest, and family life becomes more complex, the consequences of dying without having made a will become far more serious and wide reaching. This is especially true for stepfamilies.

*"Each of the parents don't want the inheritance they leave to us to end up in the hands of the ex partners and stepgrandchildren."*

Most people are concerned about the welfare of those they will leave behind. The single simple act of drawing up a will can cut out family wrangles, provide for the neediest survivors and stave off a large handout to the Inland Revenue. To emphasise the vulnerability of stepfamilies, take note of this cautionary tale.

*Cliff married Sarah when they were both 22. Very soon they had two children, Claire and Thomas. When she was 28 Sarah developed breast cancer and died three years later without ever having made a will. All her property, including money she inherited from her father, her diamond engagement ring and other jewellery and the contents of her bank account, went to Cliff.*

*Two years later Cliff fell in love with Marion who was also widowed and had two children from her first marriage, Pete and David. Six months after they met Marion became pregnant and she and Cliff got married. Their daughter Yolanda was born the following summer. On the day of Yolanda's third birthday Cliff suddenly suffered a fatal brain haemorrhage. He died without making a will and everything he owned, including all the things he'd inherited from Sarah, went to Marion.*

*Marion now had five children to bring up on her own. She was coping very well, but one day returning from collecting the children from school she was killed by a hit and run driver. Again, she left no will. As a result all her property and money passed automatically to her natural children, Pete, David and Yolanda.*

*Marion's sister, although she agreed to look after the three children, was concerned about how she would manage financially because their inheritance was tied up until they were 18 and she needed money to see them through school.*

*It was Cliff's eldest children, however, who suffered the most. Denied any inheritance at all, they had to watch their stepbrothers and half sister benefit not only from their father's wealth but their own mother's too. Claire was particularly upset to see her mother's jewellery go to her two stepbrothers Pete and David. With no money and no one who could afford to look after them, Claire and Thomas had no option but to go into local authority care, with only the hope that someone would help them make a claim under the Inheritance Act.*

Writing a will is an essential part of financial planning. Making a properly drawn-up will and taking expert advice about your tax situation needn't be expensive. Stepfamilies would be well advised to steer clear of DIY wills and see a solicitor instead.

There are three important aspects to the financial legalities of dying: the making of a will; the intestacy rules (how your assets are divided up if you don't leave a will); and the Inheritance Act (how your family and dependants can challenge the terms of your will). In addition, there are strict rules about how a will is administered, known as probate. Not surprisingly, there are also special tax regulations dealt with by inheritance tax.

# Making a will

A will is simply a document that spells out how you want to divide up your property and other assets after your death and how you want any dependent children to be provided and cared for. To be legally valid it must be properly drawn up and witnessed. Anyone who stands to benefit under your will cannot act as a witness.

---

*"We are each leaving our estates to the other and then to be divided equally between all four children – his two and my two."*

---

Your will gives you the opportunity to do a number of things including:

- divide up your estate – everything you own,
- leave special legacies – gifts or sums of money – to particular friends, relatives or charities,
- appoint the executors of your will – the people who will be responsible for administering your wishes. Banks and solicitors will do this for you but they'll make a charge,
- appoint guardians for any dependent children. You should also ensure that through your will those guardians are provided with sufficient funds to raise your children according to your wishes,
- say what kind of funeral you want and whether you wish to be buried or cremated.

Once you've made a will put it somewhere safe and tell your nearest and dearest where you've stored it.

### Changing your will

Amendments or codicils to a will also have to be properly drawn up and witnessed – no scribbling in the margins!

If you marry after making a will, then that original will is automatically revoked, that is, it has no power. Unless you make a new will you will die intestate (see below).

### Appointing guardians

As soon as a child is born it is critical that you make or amend your will. This is important for two reasons. First, a will enables you to set out who you want to care for your child in the event of your death and how you want them to do it. Second, a will enables you to make financial provision for your child and whoever is caring for them.

You can use your will to appoint testamentary guardians – the person or people who, in the event of your death, will bring up your child. You must check with whoever you wish to appoint that they are willing to undertake the task. Once they take up their duties they cannot relinquish them. Although guardians acquire parental responsibility when they take on the duty, it is not at the same level as a birth or adoptive parent.

Guardians are rarely called upon to take up their duties, and when they are this is usually done very informally. There is no need to go to court unless there is some dispute. If you don't appoint a guardian and there is no surviving birth parent or other relative able or willing to look after the child, then the local authority must take them into care.

The only people who can appoint guardians are the birth mother, the married father or the unmarried father providing he has acquired parental responsibility, an adoptive parent or someone who is already acting as a guardian. If each parent appoints a different guardian, then in the unlikely event that both parents die, the guardians will be jointly responsible for bringing up the child.

To understand the importance of appointing guardians, this is what happens when one or both of the parents dies.

### When a married parent dies
- If the mother or father dies, the survivor looks after the child and the guardian appointed by the deceased parent is disregarded.*
- If the surviving parent then dies, both guardians (if they are different) act jointly or the court appoints a guardian.

### When an unmarried parent dies
- If the mother dies, then the unmarried father looks after the child, provided that he has acquired parental responsibility* or he has been appointed guardian in the mother's will. If neither of these things has happened then the unmarried father can apply to become the child's guardian or adopt the child.
- If the father dies, then the mother continues to look after the child.*
- If the father has a residence order and he dies, then his appointed guardian looks after the child.
- If the father dies without ever having obtained parental responsibility, then his appointed guardian is disregarded.

### When a separated or divorced parent dies

- If the parent with a residence order dies, their appointed guardian looks after the child.

- If a parent who does not have a residence order for their child dies, then their appointed guardian is disregarded and the surviving parent continues to look after the child.*

### Remarried parents

- If a previously separated or divorced parent with a residence order dies, then their appointed guardian looks after the child.

- If a previously separated or divorced parent without a residence order dies, then the surviving birth parent continues to look after the child.*

In those cases marked with an asterisk (*) the right of the parent to look after the child cannot be challenged in court.

### The financial needs

It's important to get the financial provision right. Many people worry that they cannot appoint the guardians of their choice because those people's incomes are too low and taking care of the children would place an impossible burden on them. You can use your will to ensure that they have the money to help raise your child. For this reason you should take advice in drawing up trusts for your child's inheritance. You don't want to lock away all your money until your child is 18 so that the guardians are going to have to struggle financially to bring them up.

## Dying without a will

If you die intestate – without having made a will – your estate will be divided up according to the very stringent intestacy rules. These rules set down to whom your money will pass and in what proportions.

The critical thing is that they make no allowance whatsoever for your personal circumstances nor can they reflect your wishes. Most important of all, they only recognise blood relatives. There is no provision for unmarried, cohabiting partners or for stepchildren.

You also need to be aware that even your spouse will not automatically inherit your entire estate if it is worth over a certain value. Any money inherited by dependent children will be held in an inflexible trust until they are 18, which may cause financial hardship for the surviving parent or guardian.

## Challenging a will

The Inheritance Act lays down exactly who can challenge a will and the time limits within which they can do this. People usually want to a challenge a will either because they don't believe it is legally valid or they feel hard done by.

When you make a will it's worth bearing in mind that the following people can challenge it: your spouse; your former spouse who has not remarried; your children; anyone treated by you as a child of the family whether in an existing or former marriage; anyone living with you immediately before their death who was financially dependent on you.

Challenging a will is usually an extremely long drawn out and expensive process. For cohabitees the chances of success are currently very remote. As a live-in partner or simply a close friend, in order to prove you have a claim you will need to show that you were being maintained by your partner just before they died. Applications from traditional relationships where the woman undertook the housewife's role while the man paid the bills are likely to be more successful. The irony is, however, that the more care you provide, for example nursing a sick partner, in return for a roof over your head, the less likely you are to succeed in your challenge.

You can also use the Inheritance Act to challenge the effect of the intestacy rules, the same requirements will apply.

## Inheritance tax

It doesn't take much these days to land your family and friends with a heavy tax burden when you die. If you have owned your home for a long while then its value has probably increased substantially. Add to that the value of insurance policies, pensions, jewellery and other assets, and it's not difficult to see that you might be worth a considerable sum. By wise tax planning – making the most of your IHT allowances and using PETs (see below) – you can cut down the worst of your tax liabilities.

Inheritance tax (IHT) is a tax on gifts. Its name is slightly misleading because you can pay the tax both on gifts you make during your lifetime as well as those you make after your death. Although normally the donor is liable for the tax bill, in certain cases the beneficiary will have to pay up. Like other taxes, IHT has a tax-free zone.

## IHT during your lifetime

Most lifetime gifts are in fact exempt from IHT for the following reasons. To begin with, most outright gifts are known as Potentially Exempt Transfers (PETs). To count as a PET, the donor must not retain any benefit in the gift. For example, you couldn't give your house to your child and then continue to live in it – unless you paid a market rent. To make sure that the gift remains totally free of IHT you'll have to survive for at least seven years.

You can also make tax-free small gifts to individual friends and relatives. There is, however, an upper limit on the total value of gifts you can give without being landed with an IHT bill. Gifts to charities are usually also free of IHT.

And of course, lifetime gifts between spouses don't attract IHT. So you can continue giving lavishly to your husband or wife without worrying about the tax implications!

## IHT after your death

When you die, you will be regarded as having given away your entire estate and therefore everything you own will be subject to IHT. The IHT comes out of the estate. If you made any PETs in the seven years before your death then the beneficiary will have to pay IHT on those.

However, there is a very large tax-free zone for IHT. For the 1995/6 tax year this tax free allowance is £154,000. Don't forget that if your entire estate is passing to your spouse then they won't have to pay tax on their inheritance. The real tax crunch comes when the surviving spouse then dies and the estate passes to other relatives or friends. IHT is payable at 40% on the value of your estate when you die and on a sliding scale (20-40%) on the value of gifts made within seven years of your death (IHT is payable at 20% on other lifetime gifts). That's why it is so important to plan ahead.

Stepfamilies need to be especially careful in drafting their wills to ensure that their estate passes to the people they really intend should benefit, particularly where there are children from a number of relationships. For this reason you should always seek professional advice.

## Cohabitees

1. Making a will is absolutely critical for living-together couples. Unless you do so, there is no guarantee that your partner (and their children) will be provided for after your death. In particular, you should ensure that you use your will to provide a roof over your partner's head after your death as well as money to live on.

2. Lesbian and gay couples are especially vulnerable when one partner dies. This is due not so much to the law but to the current social climate and the way the law may be interpreted. A will stating how you want your funeral organised as well as making provision for the surviving partner could stave off a good deal of anguish. This is particularly true in families when the nature of your relationship has been denied or hidden. Without a will it is possible that the deceased's family may take over all the arrangements including disposing of household property, some of which might actually belong to the survivor.

## Married couples

3. You must make a new will when you marry or remarry. If you made a will when you were single, it will be invalid the moment you exchange your wedding vows – unless you made it in anticipation of the marriage.

4. Don't be lulled into a false sense of security and presume that when you die if you haven't made a will all your property will automatically go to your spouse. The intestacy rules lay down a statutory inheritance. After that any remaining wealth will pass to children, parents and other relatives in very strict order.

5. If you have children from a previous relationship you cannot make a will that excludes your current spouse in order to provide for your birth children on your death. At least, you can do this, but your spouse will have the right to challenge the terms of your will (see page 126).

6. If you die intestate before a decree absolute is granted, even if you have already been granted a decree nisi, all your property will go to your spouse. So, if you're in the middle of divorce proceedings review your will or if you don't have one – draft one.

7. If you have divorced your spouse and subsequently remarried you are not entitled to a claim to your ex-spouse's estate. If you remain single then you also may not be successful if you have already been properly provided for by the divorce settlement.

**Parenting**

8. An unmarried mother who wants to ensure that the father of her child cares for the child if she dies must either ensure that the father acquires parental responsibility (see page 61) or make the father the child's guardian in her will.

9. If you have children from a number of relationships then you may well want to provide for them differently. It can be especially difficult to arrive at an equitable although not necessarily equal distribution of your wealth. The 'pecuniary push-me, pull-you' prioritising exercise on page 46 may help you get your thoughts together. You can use your will to explain how you reached your decision.

---

*"Making our wills has proved to be difficult. My husband feels we should favour our youngest child as she will inherit only from us. I cannot agree."*

---

10. If you have birth children and stepchildren be careful how you draft your will. Should you leave your estate simply to your 'children', you may not find that your money ends up in the right hands or at least in the right proportions.

*Maggie and Julian had each been married three times. Maggie had two children from her first marriage and two from her second marriage. Since both of Maggie's husbands had died, Julian had agreed that they should adopt her children. In addition, Julian had twins by a woman with whom he had an adulterous relationship about ten years after he married Maggie. Julian was very concerned about the welfare of the twins and in his will he left a sizeable sum of money to 'my children'. By the time Julian died the adopted children had all grown up and had families of their own, while the twins were still young teenagers. However, the wording of Julian's will meant that instead of his money going to the twins as he intended it was divided up between all of the six children.*

11. The same applies if you have children or stepchildren who have been legitimated (see page 126) - and that includes adopted children. This is tremendously important because inheritance depends on seniority. For inheritance purposes, the date which counts is the one on which you were legitimated, not the date on which you were born.

*Cara and Giorgio had five children between them. Giorgio had a son, Ricardo, from his first marriage and Cara had three girls, Rachel, Leonie and Zoe, by her former husband. Subsequently Cara and Giorgio had another son, Paolo. After Paolo was born, Cara and Giorgio adopted Ricardo. When Giorgio died some years later he left most of his money to his 'youngest child'. What he meant to do was to provide for his son Paolo. What actually happened was that the money went to Ricardo, despite the fact he was now an adult. This was because Ricardo was adopted after Paolo's birth which in legal terms made him the younger child. Ricardo, not surprisingly, was reluctant to give up his inheritance and Cara had to embark on a long and expensive legal battle to gain money for Paolo. In the long term the brothers had no more contact with each other.*

12. If you don't provide for a dependent stepchild in your will, they may be able to challenge the will after your death (see page 126).

13. As a step-parent, even if you have a residence order you will not be able to appoint a guardian for your stepchild unless you have adopted them or you are already their legal guardian (see page 124).

14. Grandparents should be particularly careful to make a will and name any grandchild they wish to benefit in order to avoid any confusion. This is particularly true where a grandchild is adopted by a former son- or daughter-in-law and their new partner. Legally the grandchild is no longer considered a blood relation. Therefore any reference to 'grandchildren' would exclude this child, and they would not benefit under the intestacy rules in the absence of a will.

15. Grandparents who are concerned about leaving their wealth to their children could consider leaving it in a trust for their grandchildren. This would allow trustees of their choice to administer the funds for the benefit of the grandchildren. However, this kind of scheme may be expensive to set up and run.

16. Don't forget that you should always alter your will when your circumstances change. If you do want to change your will, make sure that you get professional advice and that the changes are drawn up and witnessed in the proper way.

# INCOME FROM STATE BENEFITS

It is impossible to go into great detail regarding the social security system. The rules and regulations change with alarming regularity and establishing and disputing claims can be a small-print nightmare. Below are the bare bones of how the system works and also some basic information about the key benefits. Please note that not all the qualifications and exclusions relating to each benefit are listed.

Because the system is so complex you should always seek advice (see below) about the most effective 'benefit package' for you. Many benefits have a knock-on effect and where you find yourself entitled to two overlapping allowances you may be better off taking one rather than the other.

To get detailed information obtain a copy of one of the CPAG (Child Poverty Action Group) annual publications listed in Part Four. They should be available for reference at your local library and all advice centres should have a copy. Alternatively seek information directly from the local office of the Benefits Agency or your local advice centre.

The social security system is made up of two components:

Non-means-tested benefits. Some of these are contributory and are paid for through your National Insurance Contributions (NICs). The rest are non-contributory and you don't need to have paid NICs to qualify.

Means-tested benefits for workers on low incomes and non-workers with little or no income.

## Non-means-tested benefits

These benefits exist to meet two needs:

- to compensate you for loss of earnings due to unemployment, sickness, pregnancy or old age. These are known as earnings replacement benefits,

- to provide special help, regardless of your working status, because you have children or are disabled.

Provided that you meet the qualifying criteria and, in the case of contributory benefits, have paid sufficient National Insurance Contributions (NICs), you will automatically qualify for the benefit. There will be no investigation of your financial circumstances.

**Watch out!** The basic rule is that you only qualify for one earnings replacement benefit at a time. In other words, you couldn't for example claim both unemployment benefit and maternity allowance.

### Time limits

Some earnings replacement benefits, namely unemployment benefit, sickness benefit, maternity allowance and widow's payment, are short-term allowances only. All the other non-means-tested benefits, both contributory and non-contributory, will be paid so long as you continue to satisfy the qualifying conditions. There are strict time limits in which you must apply for the benefits and these vary considerably between the different benefits.

Non-means-tested benefits fall into five categories, related to work, children, illness and disability, retirement and widows.

### Work-related benefits

#### Unemployment benefit

Unemployment benefit (UB) is basically a daily allowance, which means that in theory you should be 'signing on' every day. In practice you'll probably be required to sign on once a fortnight. You should normally sign on the very first day you are out of work, otherwise you may lose out. In a few cases you will be able to claim UB even if you are working. UB is payable for a year.

To claim UB you must be capable of work, in other words not ill, disabled or legally disqualified from employment because of your immigration status. In addition you must be available for work as an 'employed earner', which means that you have to be willing to work for someone else and not just as a self-employed person. You will also need to show that you are actively seeking employment and will be asked to show evidence of this.

You will not be entitled to UB if you were dismissed from your job for misconduct or you left your job voluntarily. UB is subject to tax. Tax is not deducted while benefit is being paid, but it reduces the refund you would otherwise receive through PAYE when you return to work.

From April 1996 UB and Income Support (see page 137) for people who are out of work will be replaced by a new benefit to be called Jobseeker's Allowance. This will be non-means-tested for the first six months. After that it will only be paid if you pass a means test.

### Maternity pay and benefits

There are two types of benefit. Statutory Maternity Pay (SMP) is paid by employers to women who qualify. Maternity Allowance is paid by the Benefits Agency to women who have paid sufficient contributions but who are self-employed or don't qualify for SMP.

SMP is paid at two rates, depending on how long you have worked for your employer and how many hours you work each week. If you work for two employers and you satisfy the qualifications with both, then you can claim SMP from each of them. You will have to pay tax and NICs on any benefit you receive. Maternity Allowance, on the other hand, is not taxable.

### Child-related benefits

### Child benefit

This is paid to anyone who cares for a child under 16 or under 19 and in full-time education. Only one person is entitled to claim child benefit for any one child. Benefit is paid at slightly higher rate for the first child; subsequent children receive a lower rate. Child benefit is not taxable.

You will not be entitled to claim child benefit if your child is in paid work for more than 24 hours a week, entitled to income support in their own right, or in hospital for more than 12 weeks. You will receive child benefit if your child attends a boarding school.

### One parent benefit

You can claim this if you are already receiving child benefit and you are not living with the parent of the child. One parent benefit is only paid once – you can't claim for each child. If you are in receipt of – as opposed to simply entitled to – some other benefits you may not be able to claim one parent benefit as well. Again, this benefit isn't subject to tax.

### Guardian's Allowance

If you care for a child who is effectively an orphan because their parents have both died, or one is dead and the other cannot be traced or is serving a long-term prison sentence, you can claim the Guardian's Allowance. You will have to satisfy the usual criteria about the child's age and so on.

Step-parents don't count as a parent. Therefore you may be able to claim this allowance in respect of a stepchild whose natural parents both fall into one of the categories above. You can get this benefit in addition to one parent benefit.

### Illness- and disability-related benefits

**WATCH OUT!**

**Watch out!** Concern about expenditure on sickness and invalidity benefits has led to a gradual tightening up on evidence to support claims. Added to that, from April 1995 sickness and invalidity benefits have been replaced by a new allowance called Incapacity Benefit.

### Statutory Sick Pay and Incapacity Benefit

The majority of people who are off work because of illness receive Statutory Sick Pay (SSP) paid for by their employers. Those who are not entitled to SSP receive short-term Incapacity Benefit (IB) at the lower rate, which is paid for by the Benefits Agency. Both benefits run for a maximum of 28 weeks after which, if you're still unable to work, you will receive IB but at the short-term higher rate. If you continue to be unable to work after a year you will get long-term Incapacity Benefit.

Don't confuse SSP with any occupational sickness scheme. SSP, like Statutory Maternity Pay, is simply a government-set minimum benefit, and many employers offer workers enhanced schemes.

If you're not entitled to claim SSP or IB – because you've not paid enough contributions – then you will not receive any benefit for the first 28 weeks of your illness unless you apply and qualify for the means-tested Income Support. SSP is taxable, lower-rate IB is not.

### Severe Disablement Allowance

If you are not entitled to Incapacity Benefit, because for example you've not paid enough contributions, but you remain unable to work after 28 weeks, then you may receive the Severe Disablement Allowance (SDA). This is also a long-term benefit.

### Disabled Living Allowance

Unlike sickness benefit and invalidity benefits, the Disabled Living Allowance (DLA) is a non-contributory benefit. It is also not linked to your capacity to work. Benefit is paid at different rates depending on the extent of your disability, and the DSS lays down very strict rules about proving disability.

DLA comprises a mobility component and a care component. Children under five are not entitled to the mobility part of the allowance but may be able to claim the care component. People whose care needs begin when they're over 65 can claim Attendance Allowance instead of DLA.

### Invalid Care Allowance

This is a benefit for people who are responsible for caring for someone in receipt of the higher or middle rates of the care component of DLA or attendance allowance. You cannot claim ICA if you work (although some of your earnings will be disregarded) or are in full-time education. If you are over pensionable age, you are only entitled to claim ICA if you were in receipt of it before you reached 60 or 65.

### Retirement benefits

*(See also the section on the State pension starting on page 109.)*

Retirement pensions are payable to men over 65 and women over 60. However, any woman born after 5 April 1955 will not be able to claim retirement pension until she is 65. There are three categories of pension:

- Category A is based on your contribution record,
- Category B is based on your spouse's contribution record,
- Category D is a non-contributory pension payable to those over 80.

NB Unless you're over 105 or you're a widow and your husband would be more than 110 if he was still living, don't worry about the missing Category C!

There are special rules for people who have been divorced or widowed, and these are explained more fully on page 66. If you want a state retirement pension then you need to claim it, it won't turn up automatically.

In addition, there is a series of add-on benefits such as Income Support, help with housing costs, special loans and premiums for people in certain circumstances.

### Benefits for widows

If your husband dies you may be entitled to a series of benefits. In order to make a claim your husband will have had to satisfy the contribution requirements or have died as a result of an industrial accident or disease. The benefits are aimed at women under pensionable age.

The first benefit is the <u>Widow's Payment</u> which is a lump sum payment. This is not the same as a funeral grant from the social fund.

The second benefit is the <u>Widowed Mother's Allowance</u>. You can get this if you're pregnant or you already have a child for whom you're claiming child benefit. As a stepmother you may also be able to claim for a child for whom your husband was receiving child benefit immediately before his death.

The third related benefit is the <u>Widow's Pension</u>. The amount you will receive will vary according to the age at which you were widowed and the exact amount of your husband's contribution record.

Remember, if you remarry or start cohabiting with a new partner then your entitlement to widow's benefit is likely to be affected.

## Means-tested benefits

As their name implies, means-tested benefits are allowances which you receive only after a rigorous financial investigation.

Most benefits have very complicated rules for assessing your needs and your resources in order to establish the level of your entitlement. However, some benefits, like Income Support, provide you with an automatic 'passport' to other benefits such as maternity and funeral expenses, free prescriptions, school meals and so on. There are also a number of discretionary grants and loans from something called the Social Fund. These are assessed on the merits of each individual case.

Most of the main benefits are calculated by first working out how much you need to survive on each week. This is assessed according to set amounts laid down by the government based on whether you are married or single, look after dependants, have a disability, etc. The Benefits Agency will then look at your income and resources. Part of your income and capital may be disregarded. However, if you have too much capital you may not be eligible for any benefits at all, or your entitlement may be reduced. The calculations for Housing Benefit and Council Tax Benefit are slightly more complex.

If you are receiving a non-means-tested benefit, for example Unemployment Benefit, you may also be entitled to claim a means-tested allowance such as Income Support.

**Watch out!** Benefit rates are usually uprated every April. If you are considering making a claim in the Spring, you may be better off waiting until the new rates are announced. This is because some benefit rates are fixed for a certain period from the time when you first sign on. Even if the benefit rate goes up, you may not receive an immediate increase.

**WATCH OUT!**

Here are brief descriptions of the main types of means-tested benefits.

### Non-discretionary benefits for people not in full-time work

#### Income Support

Income Support (IS) is the key benefit for people on a low income. You can make a claim if you're in part-time work – less than 16 hours a week – but not if you or your partner is a full-time worker. Once you're in receipt of IS you automatically qualify for health and education benefits. IS includes an amount to repay the interest – but not the capital – on your mortgage. If you rent your home you can claim Housing Benefit (see page 138).

Since neither you nor your partner must be in full-time work, you can make a claim on behalf of your family unit – in other words, your spouse or live-in partner and any children for whom you are responsible.

**Watch out!** If you receive, or could make a claim for, maintenance from a former spouse or partner, then any application for Income Support will immediately trigger an intervention by the Child Support Agency (see page 83).

**WATCH OUT!**

### Non-discretionary benefits for people in full-time work

#### Family Credit

Family Credit (FC) is the key benefit for low-paid workers with children. It's tax free and its aim is to provide a top-up for your wages. If you have a disability you would probably be better off claiming the Disability Working Allowance (see below).

If you're entitled to FC then you may also get housing benefit (but not help with mortgage payments) and council tax benefit. FC also helps you to qualify for certain health service and education benefits – although not free school meals.

FC is awarded on a 26-week cycle. With a few exceptions, if your circumstances change during this period – your income goes up or down or you have another child – your benefit will not be altered.

### Disability Working Allowance

This works on much the same principle as FC except that it's for low-paid workers with a disability. Once you've got the Disability Working Allowance (DWA) you can claim a disability premium on housing benefit and council tax benefit. Again, DWA normally continues for a 26-week period regardless of any changes in your circumstances.

### Other benefits

### Housing costs

You can get help with your housing costs in one of two ways. If you pay rent or live in board and lodging or in a hostel and are eligible you will normally receive Housing Benefit (HB). This is paid by your local authority and not by the Benefits Agency. You may be entitled to HB even if you do not qualify for other benefits, as the rules and regulations for calculating entitlement are more generous. You do not have to be unemployed to claim HB.

Other housing costs, like mortgage interest repayments, service charges and ground rent, are met as part of your IS calculation.

Council Tax Benefit (CTB), like HB, is paid by your local authority. If you satisfy the initial entitlement criteria – and again, the savings and capital allowances are on a more generous scale than some of the other basic benefits – the amount of benefit or rebate you will receive will be determined by your income, the number of people in your family, including any dependent children, and your total council tax bill.

### Social Fund payments

There are two kinds of Social Fund payments. The first are payments available by right. Basically if you already receive IS, FC or DWA, then provided that you satisfy any individual criteria for each of the payments you will be entitled to the benefit. However, there are some exceptions. While those on IS, FC and DWA will be entitled to Maternity Expenses Payments (a lump sum payment at a standard rate), Cold Weather Payment eligibility is tighter and is restricted to people on IS. On the other hand, those on HB and CTB also qualify for Funeral

Expenses Payments. So you see, it is quite a complicated system and you should always check out your entitlements.

In addition, the Social Fund can provide discretionary grants and loans. Budget restrictions mean that it can be very difficult to get one of these special loans, but if you have nowhere else to turn for money, then it is always worth making an application.

### What else?

There are also a range of other benefits to help meet the costs of, for example, dental treatment, fares to hospital, transport to school, school uniforms and house renovation.

**Watch out!** Claiming benefits can be an incredibly time-consuming and frustrating business. It's always worth finding out exactly what you might be entitled to before you go along to your local Benefits Office. You can do this by going to see your local advice centre. If you think you've been short changed by the Benefits Agency, question your assessment. If necessary, ask about and follow the review and appeals procedures. Don't give up!

WATCH OUT!

## STEP WATCH

### Cohabitees

1. There are fairly tight definitions about what constitutes a cohabiting couple. Essentially you need to be living together, not just under the same roof but in what is described as the same household. This means, for example, that you cook and eat together and pool all or some of your finances. In addition, the relationship should be stable, not just an occasional liaison. If you each have a separate address, then you will not be treated as a cohabiting couple.

2. Remember that the joint benefit for a couple is less than the benefit paid to two single people. If for some reason you find yourself being assessed as a couple, when in fact you're not, you should challenge the decision. This could arise where, for example, you share your home with a friend of the opposite sex or you live with someone in order to share your household expenses and provide mutual support. You can also challenge the ruling if you split up from your partner but remain under the same roof but not in the same household (see above).

# STEP WATCH continued

### Married Couples

3. Once you marry and become a couple your spouse's income and capital will be taken into account when making any benefit calculation.

4. If you are already on benefit you will obviously also be able to make a claim for your new partner if they too are out of work or on a low income. However, if you've been relying on a lone parent premium, you will of course no longer be eligible for that.

5. If your husband dies, then you may be able to claim one of the non-means-tested benefits reserved for widows. If you are already claiming benefits then your position may change and you should inform the Benefits Agency as soon as possible.

6. If you remarry and had previously been receiving a Widow's Pension, then that will obviously cease to be paid.

### Children

7. As soon as you have a child, don't forget to claim child benefit. If you claim late you will probably get up to six months in arrears. Remember to ensure that you or your partner claim for any stepchild who lives with you.

8. If you are raising your child or stepchild alone, don't forget to also claim one parent benefit. You will still qualify even if you live with a partner, provided that they are not the parent of the child. If you are in receipt of other benefits, this may affect your entitlement.

9. If you are making a claim for a means-tested benefit (see page 136) your child's capital will not count as belonging to you. However, if they have more than £3000 then you will not get benefit for that child. Lone parent and family premiums will still apply in certain cases. If you aren't entitled to claim for the child, then any income they derive from their capital won't be counted as belonging to you either. If the child's money is tied up in some kind of trust fund to which they have no access then that cash won't count.

10. Any maintenance paid to your child or your stepchild, or directly to you on their behalf, will form part of your income calculation for benefit calculation purposes.

11. A stepchild living with a step-parent will not normally be entitled to claim Housing Benefit. This is because they are regarded as a 'close relative'. However, if the stepchild previously paid rent to the step-parent, then they should challenge the decision.

# HOME OWNING

For the majority of people, buying a home is their single greatest financial undertaking. However, on a relative pound-for-pound basis many householders complete the transaction with not much more thought than they would commit to buying a three-piece suite. Yet the financial and legal consequences of owning and paying for a home have tremendous and far-reaching implications for your and your family's future security.

## The law on property ownership

In order to appreciate your legal relationship to the home you own or share with your partner, you need to grasp three legal concepts: legal title, beneficial ownership, and trusts.

- <u>Legal title</u>. The person or people whose names appear on the Land or Charge Certificate or title deeds of the property have legal title to that property – in other words, they own it.

- <u>Beneficial ownership or equitable title</u>. This is quite distinct from legal ownership. Although the law presumes that whoever owns the legal title also has beneficial ownership, it is possible to acquire beneficial ownership even if your name does not appear on the title deeds. If you acquire beneficial ownership you have the right to profit from the sale of the property and you may also have rights of occupation.

- <u>Trusts</u>. This is the means by which someone who does not own legal title can obtain beneficial ownership. A trust must be in writing and should be drawn up by a solicitor. Even if you have nothing in writing, you may be able to claim beneficial ownership through an implied trust.

To help make some sense of all this, here is how and why these legal three concepts came about.

The law on property ownership has developed and extended over the years to meet new demands created by social change. To begin with common law laid down very strict rules about property ownership based on who had legal title to – owned – the land. However, this effectively barred women and children from owning property because they couldn't hold legal title to land.

In order to get round this, the Court of Chancery came up with a second set of rules, known as equity. These made a distinction between the legal title and beneficial ownership. This meant that while one person owned the legal title to the property, in practice they held it for the benefit of someone else.

The legal mechanism used for establishing beneficial ownership is known as a trust. Quite simply one person holds the property in trust for another. This kind of trust is called an express trust because it is signed and sealed in the form of a trust deed.

A new problem then arose. As the twentieth century progressed there was a new breed of working women who were contributing towards buying and paying for the marital home. However, although by this time married women were able to hold legal title to property in their own right, most homes remained in the husband's name only. The law was quite simple: whoever held legal title owned the home. Consequently, if the marriage broke up the woman was not entitled to a share of the house regardless of her financial contributions.

**WATCH OUT!**

To protect married women a new type of trust, called an implied trust, was developed. Unlike the rest of property law it doesn't rely on a written agreement and its purpose was to enable the Divorce Court to award a proportion of the beneficial ownership of the family home to the wife.

### Co-owning your home

If you hold legal title to your home it will be as the sole owner or as a co-owner, either with your partner or other people.

There are two ways you can co-own a home – as joint tenants or as tenants in common. While both give you the same rights to occupy the property, what happens to the proceeds of the property when you sell it will depend on the kind of tenancy you have agreed.

(In this context, the words tenant and tenancy simply mean owner and ownership and have nothing to do with tenanted or rented property.)

- Joint tenants. This means that when you sell the property any proceeds will be divided equally between you. When you die your half of the property will automatically pass to your co-owner.

- Tenants in common. Under this agreement the proceeds of the property are apportioned according to the terms of the co-ownership. This gives you the opportunity to split the co-ownership in a way that best reflects the amount each party puts into buying and refurbishing the property and contributing to the mortgage repayments. When you die your share of the property will be distributed under the terms of your will, or according to the intestacy rules if you die without having made a will.

## Renting your home

The law relating to letting and renting property is another particularly complex area. It is also an extremely political one. If you have any kind of concern about your rights, either as a landlord or a tenant, you should obtain specialist advice immediately. You should see a solicitor who is an expert in this area of the law or visit your local Housing Advice or Law Centre. A Citizen's Advice Bureau might also be able to give you some simple information and point you in the right direction.

### Are you secure?

As a tenant your rights to remain in your home will depend on who your landlord is and what kind of agreement you have signed.

The majority of rented housing in Britain is provided by local authorities and housing associations. If you rent from either of these sources then you will probably have either a secured or an assured tenancy and will not be able to be evicted without good reason – for example not paying your rent.

If you rent from a private landlord then you may be more vulnerable. So long as you have either a protected or an assured tenancy then you should be secure. If you have neither of these then your rights may be very limited.

Even if you do not have security of tenure, a landlord cannot simply throw you out of your home without following the proper legal procedure and obtaining a special court order. If you are ever threatened with eviction or your landlord tries to harass you, you should seek legal advice immediately.

### Tenants' rights

You will only be responsible for paying the rent if your name appears on the rent book. Unless you are married, only the person whose name appears on the tenancy agreement or rent book has the right to occupy the property.

---

## STEP WATCH

*(Also have a look at page 148 on mortgages.)*

**Cohabitees**

1. If you and your partner intend to buy a home together without getting married, make sure that both your names appear on the title deeds. This is the securest way of safeguarding both your rights to occupy the property and ensuring that one person cannot sell it over the other's head.

2. If you are moving into your new partner's home then you can provide greater security for your family by asking your partner to transfer the legal title to you so that you both have a share in the property. Don't get caught in the trap of saying 'I'll pay the bills, you pay the mortgage'. In deciding disputes about property the court is only interested in who actually paid the mortgage.

3. Remember that it's important to decide how you own your home – as joint tenants or as tenants in common. If you are joint tenants then when you die your share of the property will pass automatically to your partner, rather than as specified under the terms of your will.

4. Equally, you need to think carefully about the effect of becoming tenants in common. There is always a danger that if you are tenants in common and your share of the property passes to someone other than your partner on your death, then the survivor may be forced to sell the property in order to realise the capital for the beneficiary of the will. You can get round this by making sure you name your partner as the beneficiary. If you do find yourself in any kind of difficulty over the property, seek legal advice quickly.

5. Don't forget that even if your partner is unwilling to let you become a co-owner of their property, you can still acquire a beneficial interest in it.

**Married couples**

6. Even if you and your partner are married, it is still worth thinking about transferring the legal title and beneficial ownership into both your names if this is not already the case. This gives the currently unnamed partner some protection in the event of an acrimonious split, as the property cannot be sold without their knowledge.


# MONEY OUT: BORROWING

In an increasingly consumer-hungry world there can be few people who don't rely on a loan of some kind to see them through their monthly spending. Whether you've got a mortgage to pay for your home, an HP agreement on your car, or you use your VISA card to cover your weekly shop, you are using credit.

To help you compare the cost of various loans, the government came up with something called the Annual Percentage Rate or APR. In theory the APR provides consumers with a standard way of comparing the total cost of the various credit deals on offer. However, with an ever-growing number of variables – arrangement fees, insurance, protection policies, card fees and so on, the APR has become a far less reliable means of making any kind of sensible comparison. The government's aim is to tighten up the use of the APR in future to help borrowers establish just what kind of repayment terms they're in for. For the time being, be careful and always make sure you know exactly how much your loan is going to cost you in the end.

## Who's responsible for the loan?

The person whose name is on the loan agreement is responsible for repaying the debt. If two or more people sign up then they become jointly and severally liable. This means that if the debt isn't paid, the lender will sue each and everyone of you to ensure they get their money back. Even if you have an informal agreement among the borrowers that only one person will actually be responsible for making the repayments, if they fail to do so, each of you remains liable for the whole of the debt.

If you use credit to buy a gift for someone else, you will be responsible for paying off the debt – even if you're no longer on speaking terms with the recipient!

### Guarantors

Sometimes lenders will be concerned about the financial status of a prospective borrower and will request the name of a guarantor. If you're asked to act as a guarantor, think about it carefully first. It's far more than a formality. If the borrower defaults then you will be liable for the debt.

## Where to borrow

Here are the chief sources of credit.

### Banks and building societies

These institutions offer a range of credit options, from cards to mortgages. Unless you have an automatic overdraft facility you'll need permission from your bank manager in order to overdraw your account. The banks are now exacting high charges for unauthorised overdrafts. So if you plan to be more liberal with your accounting than you ought to be, check out not only the interest rates at which you'll be charged on your borrowings but any additional transaction costs.

### Credit cards

There are three basic types of card – bank credit cards, charge cards and store cards. In the past there have only been two bank credit card schemes in the UK – VISA and Access/Mastercard. However, cards are now being offered by many different kinds of institutions and the rules and regulations will vary.

### Bank credit cards

These bill you each month for what you have spent, and subject to a minimum payment you can pay off as much or as little as you like. The most effective way to use a credit card is to ensure you pay up in full each month. Using your credit card as an unauthorised loan or overdraft will probably be more expensive than going directly to your bank. A word of caution – if you do intend to settle up in full make sure that you pay on time. One day late and you could have to pay interest on your entire month's spending.

## Charge cards

Unlike bank credit cards, these require you to pay off your account in full each month. Charge card holders pay a joining fee plus a yearly fee, but there's no credit limit. Examples are American Express and Diner's Card.

## Store cards

These can be option accounts which are similar to bank credit cards; monthly accounts which operate like charge cards; and budget accounts where you can borrow a multiple of an agreed monthly payment.

Before you take out a store card check that it wouldn't be cheaper to charge your purchases to your regular credit or charge card. For large buys you might be better off with an agreed overdraft or personal loan from your bank.

## Credit from shops

Shops and chain stores are increasingly offering credit sales. These agreements are usually for fairly short periods – six months to a year. A shop or dealer may also arrange a finance company personal loan, especially for larger purchases such as a car. If you are offered this kind of loan, you're entitled to shop around to see if you can get a better deal elsewhere – and it's usually worth the effort.

## Hire purchase

One of the more expensive forms of credit, HP is usually offered by individual shops. You pay for the item by instalments, usually at a fixed rate throughout the agreement. You only legally own the item when you've paid your last instalment.

If you find yourself in difficulties then you can end the agreement by paying at least half the total amount payable (unless your agreement says otherwise) and returning the goods to the shop.

## Pawnbrokers

Pawnbrokers have made a very respectable comeback on the high street. For small, very short-term loans they can be useful – but expensive. If you borrow from a pawnbroker then they must follow very strict procedures and give you a proper receipt called a 'Notice to Debtor'. Read this carefully because it sets out your rights to reclaim the pawned articles.

### Moneylenders

Moneylenders often make loans where no one else will. Consequently they are likely to charge you extremely steep rates – and they can be less than scrupulous when it comes to recovering unpaid debts. It's an offence to stop someone on the street and offer them a loan or to call uninvited at a home address. Most moneylenders need a licence, so contact your local Trading Standards Department if you have any doubts.

## Secured loans

Many lenders will ask you for security when you request a loan. Often they will ask for your home as security, or perhaps a car or other valuable item. This means that if you default on your repayments then whatever you have given as security may be sold to raise money to repay the loan. Mortgage lenders will obviously require your house as security, but in other circumstances avoid giving your home. People have been known to lose the roof over their head for really quite small debts – and it's simply not worth it.

## Mortgages

Before you search around for a mortgage you need to think about the following: the total amount you're going to have to pay out each month; how much of a risk you can afford to take; and what kind of flexibility your mortgage scheme offers you. The range of mortgage packages and tie-ins is becoming increasing sophisticated and it is really worth getting some good financial advice before you sign up.

There are three basic types of mortgage available: repayment, endowment and pension.

### Repayment mortgages

This is the least risky of all mortgages, because so long as you make all your repayments the mortgage is guaranteed to be paid off. Your monthly payment goes to pay off both the capital you have borrowed and the interest which has accrued on it. Most lenders will insist that you take out an additional life insurance or mortgage protection policy to ensure that the debt is paid off if you die.

It's possible to get level repayment mortgages where your basic monthly payment after tax stays the same throughout the life of the mortgage – except for interest rate changes. You can also get increasing payment mortgages where the repayments start off low and then increase.

One word of caution on repayment mortgages: if you tend to move regularly, say every five years or so, remember that to start with most of your monthly payment goes on repaying the interest. Therefore in a five-year period the actual size of your capital debt will hardly have reduced. Every time you move and take out a new repayment mortgage, the process starts again and very little is actually paid off.

## Endowment mortgages

You make two monthly payments: one goes to pay off the interest on the loan; the other pays for the premiums on an investment-linked life insurance policy. The idea is that when the policy matures at the end of the mortgage term the returns can be used to pay off the loan and will hopefully provide you with an extra lump sum.

Endowment mortgages come in two varieties, either the traditional with-profits policy or the more risky unit-linked endowment policies. With the latter there's no guarantee what the policy will be worth when it matures. As with all unit-linked schemes its value will depend on the ups and downs of the economy.

There is some risk that the proceeds of a traditional with-profits policy may not be sufficient to repay the whole of your mortgage. In calculating the amount you need to save, most lenders make the assumption that bonuses will accrue on your policy (see page 108). However, if in fact they accrue at a lower rate than the lender originally assumed, perhaps because investments performed poorly, there may not be sufficient to repay your mortgage. Lenders normally review your contributions periodically to stop this happening and you may be asked to increase your monthly payments. The only way you can be sure of avoiding this risk is by saving enough so that the minimum guaranteed return equals your mortgage, but this may be prohibitively expensive.

## Pension mortgages

Working along the same principle as endowment mortgages, part of your monthly payment will pay off the interest on the loan and the rest will go to make tax-free contributions to an approved pension scheme. When you eventually take your pension you use part of it as a tax-free lump sum to repay your mortgage.

You can also take out a personal equity plan (PEP) mortgage. This works in exactly the same way except this time the proceeds of the PEP are used to pay off your mortgage. Again, this has tax advantages, but once more remember that you'll have no guarantee that the PEP will provide sufficient funds to repay the loan in full.

### Fixed versus variable rates

Fixed rate mortgages are becoming increasingly popular. The rates are fixed for a specified period, usually one, three or five years although you can get much longer fixed term periods. The actual rate at which the interest on the loan is fixed may vary according to the term you've agreed. The advantage of fixing all or part of your mortgage is that you can at least budget effectively since your monthly repayment will not be affected by fluctuations in interest rates.

However, there is one point you should bear in mind. Although most lenders will allow you to take a fixed rate mortgage with you when you move, if you repay the loan before the fixed term is up you may suffer very heavy penalties. If you intend to move abroad, go into the rented sector or want the freedom to change your mortgage to your next property, make sure that you don't agree to fix the mortgage for longer than the time you intend to live in your current home.

WATCH OUT!

**Watch out!** If you're planning to move home, don't forget to include in your calculations all the up-front costs such as arrangement fees for your mortgage, stamp duty, search and land registry fees, conveyancing costs, estate agents' fees, plus removal and any utility connection costs. These can all add up to very serious money and they need to be paid more or less on the day you move.

## STEP WATCH

### Cohabitees

1. Whether you are the legal co-owner or you have acquired a beneficial interest in your home, a mortgage lender will usually insist that your name appears as a joint mortgagee. This means that whatever arrangement you have between you to repay the mortgage, you will each be liable for the whole of the debt.

2. If your name does not appear on the mortgage then you are not responsible for repaying the loan. The lender cannot pursue you for any arrears, but neither do they have to notify you of them.

3. If you have a legal and beneficial interest in the property and you find that the lender is about to take action to repossess the property because your partner has not been paying up, you can ask to be made party to the proceedings. This means that you can ask the lender to allow you to remain in the house provided you continue to make the repayments.

### Married couples

4. However, if the property is in the name of one spouse who defaults on repaying the mortgage, the building society or other lender must accept repayments from the other spouse. If this problem arises you should consult your mortgage lender immediately.

5. Mortgages cannot simply be transferred from one spouse to another, or to anyone else for that matter. In divorce proceedings the court can only order the transfer of a property subject to the lender agreeing to the transfer of the mortgage. Unless and until the lender does so, the person with whom the mortgage was originally agreed will remain liable for the debt.

6. If you have an endowment mortgage (see page 149) you should also make sure that you apply to transfer the beneficial interest in the insurance policy. If you don't do this, you may find that whichever one of you takes on the mortgage may not have sufficient to pay off the loan when the term is up.

### General

7. You may decide that one person should legally own the house while the other remains primarily responsible for the mortgage. There are a number of reasons why you might want to do this. For example, where the husband is selfemployed he may prefer that his wife is the sole owner of their property. This would protect the family home if his business failed and he was made bankrupt. In this case, it is usual for the lender to insist that the wife takes independent legal advice so that she understands that her home will be repossessed if her husband fails to meet the mortgage repayments.

8. If your partner dies and you are left with the property, then provided that there is appropriate life assurance, you may be able to use it to pay off any outstanding mortgage.

9. However, you will need to keep up the mortgage repayments if you are the sole owner, or you inherit the property and there was no appropriate insurance policy.

# TAX

Tax is one of the most horribly complex areas of financial law and practice. For all but the most basic planning you may need to get some expert, specialist advice either from a solicitor, accountant or financial adviser. For general background information the Inland Revenue produces a series of excellent free leaflets.

You can be taxed two ways: directly, for example by paying income tax, and indirectly when you pay VAT on things you buy or special duties such as excise duty on beer. In financial planning terms, what counts is how you manage the ways you are taxed directly.

There are three common types of direct taxation that are most likely to affect you: Income Tax (IT), Capital Gains Tax (CGT), which you pay when you dispose of a valuable asset such as a second home or work of art, and Inheritance Tax (IHT), which is a tax paid on gifts made both during your lifetime as well as on your death.

## The tax system

Personal taxes and other forms of direct taxation are collected by the Inland Revenue, which is a government department. The Inspector of Taxes and staff assess how much tax you should pay and the Collector of Taxes ensures you pay up.

You will be assigned to a tax district which will deal with all your tax affairs. However, your tax district won't necessarily be the one located nearest to you geographically. The district to which you are allocated will depend on your source of income. For example, if you're an employee or a pensioner your tax district will be the one that's responsible for the area in which your company's headquarters or wages office is situated. This means that if you change jobs, your tax district may also change.

The tax year runs from 6 April until 5 April the following year. If you have a steady income from a job or a pension which the Inspector of Taxes already knows about via your employer, then you may never receive a tax return. If, on the other hand, you're running your own business or you have investment income then you'll almost certainly be asked to complete one each year. Returns are normally sent out at the beginning of each tax year. Self-assessment is being introduced in the tax year 1996/7. For that and subsequent years you will normally have until the end of September by which to get the form back if you want the Inland Revenue to calculate your tax bill. But if you are prepared to calculate your tax bill yourself, you have until the end of January. Until the introduction of self-assessment you normally have until 31 October to fill in and send back the tax return.

The whole business of calculating and paying tax is made up of four distinct steps:

1. Establishing which of your sources of income are liable to tax.

2. Working out how much income you can earn tax free.

3. Calculating any additional tax relief you may be entitled to.

4. Assessing the rate at which you will pay tax on your taxable income after the other three steps have been carried out.

**Watch out!** It's your responsibility to tell the Inland Revenue that it has to tax you! Even if you don't receive a tax return, you must tell the Inland Revenue if your circumstances change and you have any new income or capital gains that it doesn't know about from previous returns. Equally, you must also tell the Revenue if your family situation alters.

WATCH OUT!

## Income that is liable for tax

Income tax isn't just paid on earnings from your job: interest from building society accounts, shares and other investments is also liable. You should be prepared to pay tax on income from the following sources:

- Employment. If you're an employee then you're probably on PAYE (Pay As You Earn) which means that tax will automatically be deducted by your employer.

  If you're self-employed then the rules for paying tax are slightly different. In general, you will submit a return for the profits you make in each financial year. If you're in this situation it's worth getting some professional advice on accounting procedures and effective tax planning.

- State benefits. Unemployment benefit, the State retirement pension and most other State benefits are liable for tax.

- Pensions. Retirement pensions, including a widow's pension, are liable for tax. If you're receiving a pension through your former employers then you'll usually be taxed through PAYE.

- Interest on savings and investments. Although most building societies and banks deduct basic rate tax at source, National

Savings accounts and deposits, income or capital bonds do not. You'll also have to declare any profits or dividends you've made on any shares, annuities or other investments you have.

- Other sources. If you rent out your home or any other property you own or you collect ground rents then you'll have to declare it. Any income from overseas accounts must also be declared, although there are special rules for people whose permanent home is not in the UK.

## Tax allowances

Everyone has a tax allowance or tax-free zone. How much you're entitled to will depend on your marital status and your personal circumstances. The allowance rates are set each year in the Budget. There are three main types of allowance:

- Personal allowance. You will automatically get this regardless of your sex or your marital status. The exact amount of your allowance will depend on your age.

- Married couple's allowance (MCA). The MCA is usually claimed by the husband. However, if his income is so low that he cannot make use of all the allowance, he can transfer the excess to his wife. Alternatively, the MCA can be split equally between husband and wife. The MCA can only be set against your liability to pay tax at the rate of 15% (see below).

- Additional personal allowance. This is mainly for single parents and unmarried couples with children. There are also other special allowances, such as widow's bereavement allowance and a blind person's allowance.

## Tax relief

Another way to reduce the amount of income you have to pay tax on is by claiming tax relief on certain outgoings. The most common types of tax relief are:

- Mortgage interest relief. You can claim this if you've taken out a loan to buy your only or your main home. Most people will get this type of tax relief automatically through the MIRAS – Mortgage Interest Relief At Source – system. This makes for a very tax-efficient way of borrowing money. If your mortgage lender is not part of MIRAS you may have to claim this relief directly from your tax office.

- Tax relief on maintenance payments. However, not all types of maintenance payments qualify. Broadly, in order to claim relief the payments must be made to your former spouse for the benefit of your children. Payments directly to children or to cohabitees will not attract relief.

## Tax rates

There are currently three different rates at which tax is paid: a lower rate band, a basic rate band, and a higher rate band.

The first £3200 of your taxable income is subject to lower rate tax at 20%. The next £21,100 or less is liable to basic rate tax, which is 25%. If you still have taxable income left above that you will have to pay the higher rate tax of 40% on the remainder. (These rates are for the tax year 1995/6.)

## Capital Gains Tax (CGT)

CGT is paid whenever you dispose of an asset, whether you sell it or give it away as a gift. Assets might include a house or land – other than your main home – foreign currency, shares or valuable items such as paintings or antique furniture. However, some sales or gifts are not liable to CGT.

CGT is generally payable on the real increase in the value of the asset over inflation while you owned it. CGT is paid at the same rates as income tax.

For a start, everyone has a CGT-free zone, which means you can make a certain amount of profit or capital gain each year without having to pay tax (£6000 for 1995/6). Secondly, you won't have to pay CGT on your main home. Thirdly, gifts between spouses are exempt from CGT. In addition, you should also remember that certain types of investments are also free of CGT.

For information about Inheritance Tax see page 126.

## STEP WATCH

1. If one partner is earning and the other isn't, you might think about putting all your savings into the account of the non-earner. The non-tax-payer can then reclaim any tax already deducted from the interest earned on the savings.

   In order for this to work for tax purposes the earning partner must retain no legal or beneficial interest in the savings. This means that the account must be in the sole name of the non-earner and you must not draw up any formal agreement saying that you both have a right to the savings. This has an obvious snag if you split up. The earner will not be able to demand any money from the new account. If the non-earner doesn't want to give them a share of the money, they don't have to. However, if you cohabit with your partner and are transferring large sums, watch out that you don't incur CGT (see page 155). This won't apply, of course, if you are married.

2. Think carefully about how you use your married couple's allowance. If a husband is a non- or low earner and cannot make full use of his MCA, then he can transfer the surplus to his wife. Alternatively you can decide simply to split the MCA between you.

### Remarriage

3. If a husband is claiming the additional personal allowance (APA) for his children in the year he remarries, he must choose whether to continue with the APA or take a proportion of the married couple's allowance (MCA). You cannot benefit from both allowances at the same time.

4. However, where a wife has claimed APA for her children immediately before her remarriage, she can continue to claim it for the remainder of the tax year.

5. In the tax year following the remarriage, the husband must claim only the MCA.

### Children

6. Even a baby in nappies is liable for tax – if they earn enough! For tax purposes a child is treated as a single person and therefore receives a single person's allowance. This means that anything they earn, for example, on a paper round, is counted as income. In practice their personal allowance will probably far exceed their income and they won't have to pay tax.

7. If your child receives a grant or scholarship then that won't count as income. However, if the scholarship is paid as one of the parent's fringe benefits by their employer, then you can be taxed on it.

8. If you have a child – including stepchildren – under 16 or under 18 and in-full time education, you can claim the additional personal allowance (APA) provided that one of the following applies:

- you are a single parent,
- you are separated, divorced or widowed and have responsibility for bringing up your child.

In effect the APA replaces entitlement to the married couple's allowance. Whatever your situation, you certainly cannot claim both. In the year that a husband and wife separate, the wife, if she has care of the children, might claim APA, while the husband continues to claim MCA.

If you are cohabiting parents you can only claim one APA between you – even if you each bring to the relationship a child by a former partner.

9. Whether unmarried or married, parents who split up and share the care of their child can apportion the APA according to how much time the child spends with each parent. If you cannot decide between you how to divide the allowance, the Inland Revenue will decide for you.

### Grandparents

10. If grandparents have sufficient financial resources, gifts by them to their grandchildren can be very tax efficient. Unlike gifts from parents, any income from the investment of the gift is not attributed back to the giver.

11. Gifts during the life of the grandparent are usually PETs and free from inheritance tax (see page 126). They will also reduce the value of the grandparent's estate – and so their IHT – when they die.

### Separation

12. A husband can claim the married couple's allowance for the remainder of the tax year in which he separates.

13. If one partner buys the other out or one spouse's share in the property was given to the other as part of the financial settlement, then there may be a liability to CGT. The person who leaves the marital home may have to pay tax if they move into their new property before the old one is sold or transferred.

## Maintenance

*(The rules governing maintenance and tax have been revised. Broadly, the following information will apply to any maintenance agreements made after 15 March 1988. If you received a court order before then and you have any queries you should contact your local tax office.)*

14. To qualify for tax relief on maintenance payments, you need to satisfy the following conditions:

   - the maintenance must be the subject of a court order or other enforceable agreement,

   - the payments must be to a divorced or separated spouse and not a former cohabitee,

   - the spouse receiving the payments must not have remarried,

   - the payments must be to maintain the spouse and not the children.

   You won't get tax relief on lump sum payments.

15. You will not get any tax relief on maintenance you pay to children directly, even if they are under 21. Provided that you satisfy the other general rules, you will get tax relief if you make the payments for your children to your former spouse. If you receive maintenance payments for a child, then you will not be taxed on them.

## Bereavement

16. If a wife dies her husband can continue to claim the married couple's allowance (MCA) for the rest of the tax year in which she died.

17. If a husband dies, his widow can claim any of her late husband's MCA for the tax year in which he died, which cannot be set against the income for that tax year. She can also claim widow's bereavement allowance for the tax year of her husband's death plus the following tax year so long as she does not remarry.

# DEALING WITH MONEY PROBLEMS

Debt is one of the biggest consumer problems. For the vast majority it's not a question of irresponsible spending that lands them in the County Court. It often takes a single incident – illness, redundancy, the break-up of a marriage – to tip the scales from making ends meet to a mounting spiral of unpaid bills.

Ironically, the rise in debt has to some extent had three positive effects. First, the notion of being in debt has become more socially acceptable, and people are increasingly willing to be open about their financial difficulties. Second, lenders have become more sympathetic towards borrowers in trouble and up to a point are showing greater flexibility in repayment arrangements. Third, there is far greater awareness about some of the issues surrounding debt and more opportunities for independent help and advice.

If you find yourself in financial hot water it's absolutely vital you take some action. Ignoring the mounting pile of brown envelopes will not make the problem go away. Leave them alone to fester and you'll find yourself in a deeper financial hole out of which it'll be even harder to climb.

Even if you don't think your money problems are of your own making, venting your spleen against a wayward ex-partner, boss or child will not actually keep the bailiffs from the door. Save your energies and put them into managing your debts.

## Debt action plan

Here is a basic six-point plan to help you manage your debts. You can get specialist advice from your local Citizens Advice Centre or Money Advice Centre. There is also a national debt helpline (see Part Four).

1. <u>Don't panic</u>. Get a fresh piece of paper and write down all your outstanding financial commitments. Don't be tempted to round anything up or down, or skip over 'minor' bills. Frightening as it is to see everything in front of you in black and white, you're beginning to grasp your debts by the scruff of their necks, so hang on in there.

2. <u>Get in contact with each of your creditors</u> – banks, building societies, utility companies, finance houses, whoever they are. It's really important you let them know that you're aware you owe them money, about your current financial position, and that you intend to settle your debt. If you don't talk to them and explain your current money difficulties, you can't really blame them for assuming that you simply don't want to pay up.

A quick telephone call, followed by a brief three-sentence letter acknowledging the debt and saying that you intend to put forward an offer to settle, will suffice at this stage.

**WATCH OUT!**

**Watch out!** Your biggest creditor may not always be your priority creditor. In deciding what order you deal with them, you need to think what immediate action each can take against you. Credit card companies, for example, may cancel your card but beyond that there's not a lot they can do in the short term. Gas, electricity and telephone companies, on the other hand, have a very simple remedy – they can cut you off. And they may well make a substantial charge to reconnect you when you finally pay up. Other priority debts include unpaid fines, Council Tax, and money you owe the Inland Revenue. Above all, watch out for any loans secured on your home (see page 148).

3. If your home is at risk, see your mortgage lender immediately. Even if you are only one or two months in arrears, a reduction in or loss of income, however temporary, could have a severe knock-on effect on your ability to make future repayments. Many mortgage lenders will give you some breathing space by extending your mortgage repayment period. You also need to think realistically about the possibility of moving and reducing your mortgage, or renting. In this case it really is better to jump than be pushed. If you can keep control of the sale of your home rather than let it go under a forced mortgage repossession, the more likely you are to achieve a better price for it.

If the value of your house is less than your mortgage – negative equity – then it is particularly important to talk to your lender, as the options open to you may be severely limited.

At this stage you also ought to think very carefully before you stop making contributions to savings or pension plans. Talk to an independent adviser and check whether you are covered by an appropriate insurance scheme.

4. Make out a weekly budget excluding all your current debts and your regular mortgage repayments if you've managed to defer them (see above). Subtract your outgoings from your income. Whatever you have left is what's available to divide up between your creditors. If the kitty is almost empty, don't despair. The important thing is to be able to provide your creditors with your complete financial picture, however bleak.

5. Contact your creditors again. Write to them with an offer to settle your debt. Think about your offer very carefully. Never commit yourself to more than you can realistically pay, you'll only compound your problems. One way to work out how to pay off your various creditors is to follow this formula.

**A**

Add up all your debts

For example, Sam owes a total of £3500 which is made up as follows:

| | |
|---|---|
| Mortgage arrears: | £1000 |
| Visa card: | £ 600 |
| Finance company: | £1550 |
| Gas: | £ 75 |
| Electricity: | £ 150 |
| Telephone: | £ 125 |
| Total: | £3500 |

**B**

Now you need to work out each individual debt as a percentage of the total amount you owe. If you have a calculator you can do this simply by entering the amount of the individual debt then dividing it by the amount of the total debt and multiplying it by 100.

In Sam's case, the outstanding mortgage arrears would be calculated as follows: £1000 ÷ £3500 x 100 = 28.57%. Rounding the figures her entire calculation would look like this.

| | |
|---|---|
| Mortgage arrears: | 28.57% (29%) |
| Visa card: | 17.14% (17%) |
| Finance company: | 44.29% (44%) |
| Gas: | 2.14% (2%) |
| Electricity: | 4.28% (4%) |
| Telephone: | 3.57% (4%) |

**C**

Now you need to translate each debt percentage into a slice of real money from your weekly repayment kitty. To do this on your calculator first enter the debt percentage (without using the % key), then multiply that number by the amount of your weekly repayment kitty and finally divide by 100.

Sam has worked out that after she has met all her regular outgoings she has just under £15 left each week to pay off her outstanding debts. Her mortgage arrears calculation would therefore look like this: 29 x £15 ÷ £100 = £4.35. Sam could offer to repay her mortgage arrears at £4.35 a week. Her complete weekly repayment plan works out like this:

| | |
|---|---|
| Mortgage arrears: | £4.35 |
| Visa card: | £2.55 |
| Finance company: | £6.60 |
| Gas: | £0.30 |
| Electricity: | £0.60 |
| Telephone: | £0.60 |

With your letter to your creditor you should enclose a full statement of your weekly or monthly budget, together with a complete list of all your creditors and how much you owe each of them.

If you owe money to a credit company you may also wish to ask them to freeze the interest which will be accruing on your account. Point out to them that since you are already having problems paying your existing debt there is little point in them adding to the amount of their unpaid bill by mounting up the interest. They are more likely to be sympathetic if you can show that in the foreseeable future there is little hope of your financial circumstances improving.

6.  Once you have agreed a repayment arrangement, stick to it. If you default on the repayments your creditors are going to be far less sympathetic next time round. However, if you get into genuine difficulties, contact them immediately and explain the situation.

## Maximising your income

While you're sorting out who you owe money to and how you're going to repay it, you ought to consider whether there is any way you can increase your income. Many people could improve their cashflow, not simply by watching where their pounds go each week, but by ensuring they claim money they're actually entitled to. This is particularly true if you've lost your job or are unable to work and are relying on benefits.

There are three sources you can look to for maximising your income:

Your wages and other earnings For a start, check your wage packet: is it correct? Have you looked into overtime opportunities? If you've been dismissed from work and haven't worked out your notice period, have you had money in lieu of notice? Are your redundancy payments right? Have you claimed your entitlement to Maternity Pay?

Your tax bill Is your tax liability at its lowest possible limit? Are you sure that your tax coding is correct? Have you claimed all your tax allowances and tax reliefs? As a couple are you making effective use of your married couple's allowance (see page 154)?

State benefits If you're unemployed, on a low income, disabled or have dependent children, it's always worth checking that you're getting all the benefits you're entitled to. For example, you may be able to get a rebate on your Council Tax. If you receive Child Benefit and you're bringing up a child alone, don't forget that you are also entitled to the lone parent premium so long as you are not living with the parent of the child. If you're on Income Support or Family Credit, remember that you can claim a whole range of 'add on' benefits such as free prescriptions and dental treatment. Remember too that you may be entitled to have premiums added to your assessment for Income Support if, for example, you have a disabled child.

Whatever your circumstances, check out your benefit situation by either going to your local benefit office, visiting a Citizens Advice Bureau or reading one of the publications listed in Part Four of this book.

If you are in financial trouble, it really is so important to trawl through your income and expenditure with a very fine-toothed comb. For every amount of money entering or leaving your personal coffers, look around it and ask yourself: How can I increase this income? Does this payment have a knock-on effect? How can I lower this bill?

**Shark warning!** However bad your debt problems get, don't be tempted by the 'clear your debts' offers that regularly appear in the newspapers. The idea of swopping a myriad of debt problems for one single loan might sound enticing, but it could well be a case of out of the frying pan and into a very hot fire. For the privilege of having someone else take you on as a bad risk you will probably have to pay exorbitant interest rates and a whopping 'arrangement fee'. You'll also have to give your home as security, which if you have repayment problems could land you out on the street. If you're in this situation, seek proper debt advice. Steer well clear of the loan sharks.

## Bailiffs

As the recession bites the repossession heavies are making quite a comeback. Confronting bailiffs can be an intimidating and humiliating experience, and in the case of some of the less scrupulous operators downright frightening.

If the bailiffs are lurking like a dark shadow on your financial horizon, it's important to remember that they rarely turn up out of the blue. Their visit is usually heralded by numerous payment demands from your creditors and normally a court summons.

However, even if they are knocking at your door, they don't have the automatic right to storm your home and take whatever you possess.

If you find yourself in this situation you should seek professional advice very fast either from your solicitor or your local advice centre. In the meantime you should bear the following in mind:

- Bailiffs are employed, usually by the courts, to collect unpaid debts. They normally do this by removing enough of your possessions to pay off the debt and cover their own costs. By the time your debt crisis has reached the bailiff stage, it's just possible the original creditor has sold the debt to a company that specialises in recovering outstanding bills. Therefore the bailiff may be acting on behalf of a new, and possibly less sympathetic, creditor.

- Although bailiffs can arrive at any time, you don't have to let them into your home. However, if you physically assault them in order to stop them crossing the threshold you might be arrested. They can't legally break into your home but they can climb through or unlock partially open windows. They can also smash open locked cupboards.

- Once inside your home, they can only seize certain items. They are not allowed to take essential clothing, bedding and other basic domestic items. Nor are they allowed to remove things that are permanently attached to the walls, or the tools of your trade. They also cannot take goods which don't belong to the debtor. So, for example, if your partner had a debt, the bailiffs couldn't remove your belongings or those of your children.

- If you're not in when the bailiffs call they may push a statement of means through your letterbox. This form asks you about your financial circumstances and you should complete and return it as soon as possible. This is a good opportunity to try and negotiate a settlement with the bailiffs.

- You may be asked to sign a 'walking possession' agreement. This means that although they won't remove the goods there and then, you'll have to agree not to sell or get rid of them. You'll have to pay a fee for every day the agreement is in force.

- Once your goods have been seized you may still recover them. You will be given at least five days to settle the debt or agree a repayment schedule. Alternatively, you can apply to the court to have the bailiff's warrant suspended.

There are strict rules governing how bailiffs go about their business and how they can sell your property. If you think that a bailiff has acted improperly, you should complain to the court which sent them.

## Refused credit?

Under the Consumer Credit Act 1974 you have the right to find out and challenge information held about your creditworthiness.

Before most lenders will agree to give you credit they will want to establish whether you are a good or bad risk. To do this they use a system known as 'credit scoring'. You will be given a rating depending on your financial status, age and so on, based on the answers you give on the credit application form. The lender will have set a 'pass mark' and so long as you meet this, you should get the loan. Many lenders use special credit reference agencies to check out your financial position. However, the system can be a bit crude and mistakes happen.

If you are refused credit you should contact the supplier or finance house immediately. Find out if they used a credit reference agency and get their name and address. You should then write to the agency and ask them what information they have on you. If the information is wrong, for example if they've listed an unknown person at your address, or they claim you have a County Court judgment against you, then you can ask to have your file corrected. There are strict time limits in force. The Office of Fair Trading produces an excellent leaflet on this type of credit problem, which you can ask for at your local Trading Standards Department or advice centre.

## FINANCIAL INFORMATION AND ADVICE

(The addresses and telephone numbers of the organisations mentioned here appear in Part Four starting on page 175. For information on benefits see page 131.)

### Financial advisers

Throughout this book you'll see the magic words 'always seek independent financial advice'. But what exactly is independent advice and where can you get it?

The average high street money shopper is faced with a number of dilemmas when it comes to choosing an adviser. There are two main categories of adviser, those who are tied and those who are independent.

#### Tied advisers

Almost all the well-known banks and building societies will only sell you financial products designed or promoted by themselves or a company with which they have close links. The same applies to some financial advisers, both companies and individuals.

This means that when you or they walk through the door looking for or giving advice, you will only be told about a limited range of products. While the products that the particular institution can offer you may be right for you, there could be other products offered by their competitors which may be more beneficial. Equally, they may not be able to provide you with the best type of product to suit your needs because they don't happen to stock it. Then again, they might.

## Independent advisers

Independent advisers (those who are not tied to one particular range of products) have a duty to give advice on the best products for you chosen from whatever is available on the market. Independent advisers are usually small companies but accountants and solicitors may also offer advice. They are paid in one of two ways. They either receive commission from the company supplying the product they sell to you, or they charge you a fee.

Obviously if they work on a commission basis, there's a danger of a conflict arising between them earning their living and the quality of advice they give to you, the client. For this reason, unless you have been recommended to a particularly reputable commission-based independent adviser, you may be better off sticking with someone who will charge you a flat fee and who will refund to you any commission they receive.

As with everything else, there are tied advisers who will offer you excellent advice and those who will give you bad information. Equally, there are top-quality independent advisers and some of doubtful calibre.

Therefore, whoever you seek financial information from, you need to ask them two questions:

1. Are you or your company tied to any particular range of products, or are you able to recommend or give advice on any product currently on the market?

2. How are you remunerated?

## Finding an independent adviser

You can check whether your financial adviser really is independent by contacting the Securities and Investment Board (SIB). The Registry of Financial Planning produces a free list of independent advisers and will indicate which of them are fee based. IFA Promotions offers a consumer helpline and will send you a list of six local independent advisers for free: however, most of these will be commission based. Finally, *Money Management* magazine has a list of fee-based independent financial advisers and they'll give you names in your area for nothing.

## Other sources of information

If you want to broaden your awareness and knowledge of financial issues then the best places to turn are the personal money sections of many of the quality newspapers. Although the city and finance pages might look a bit intimidating, the once-a-week personal money sections are usually full of the latest news, gossip and advice.

ProShare, the body set up with government funding to promote wider share ownership, produces an inexpensive and useful guide on where to get more information about all aspects of investment. There are also a number of schemes around where serious private investors can get the latest information about interest rates, share issues and so on. Most of them charge you an annual fee for their publications.

## Complaining

As the personal finance industry grows so do the number of regulators. If you have a complaint you should follow this three-point plan:

1. Talk directly to the company concerned. Go to the most senior person in the company if you get no joy lower down. Always keep photocopies of any correspondence and make a note of any telephone conversations.

2. If you find you're getting nowhere, contact the relevant self-regulatory body whose name will appear at the bottom of any correspondence you've received.

3. Finally, if you're still unhappy and the regulator has been unable to solve the problem, complain to the appropriate ombudsman, if there is one.

The Securities and Investment Board can tell you which body to complain to. They also produce a series of free leaflets about investing, financial advice and what to do if things go wrong.

A full list of regulatory bodies, ombudsmen and professional organisations appears in **Part Four** on page 175.

# CONCLUSION

In a previous STEPFAMILY publication, *Parenting Threads: Caring for children when couples part*, our final message to our readers was:

<u>inform</u> those close to you about what you want, need and are going to do so that they are not left anxiously worrying and wondering

<u>communicate</u> your plans, fears, hopes and anxieties in such a way that your ex-partner, new partner, children and stepchildren feel able to offer you support for your needs but can also feel able to express their needs, which may be in conflict with yours

<u>co-operate</u> with each other as partners, as a stepfamily, as a team of people concerned about each other and who want the best possible arrangements for the children involved within the constraints or limited options available to you.

In consulting with a wide range of our members and counsellors for this book the same underlying threads of information, communication and co-operation ran through every stepfamily story. We leave you with one such contribution:

*"We were determined to make it work so even when things got tough after John's redundancy we talked and listened to each other's fears about how we would cope without his very high income that we had all got used to. It meant really listening and saying to each other 'what's important to you is important to me'. His guilt about leaving his first wife had been partly covered up by making big payments which we knew we couldn't do anymore and he was going to have to face her with this. But I also knew it would break his heart if his children turned against him. Although it had been really important to me to give up work and stay at home with our children I took a temporary job so that we had some extra money coming in. John had to do more around the house and with the children but it gave both families time to adjust to living on a lot less. She found a part-time job and then six months later John was offered a position locally so it has all worked out. But those were difficult times when we could have all been angry with each other rather than trying to find a solution that was good enough."*

Stepfamilies and remarriage are clearly a re-investment in family life but usually on limited resources. Making the best possible use of what you have is clearly in everyone's interest.

**For further information, advice and support about stepfamily matters you can contact:**

**STEPFAMILY,**
**Chapel House, 18 Hatton Place,**
**London EC1N 8RU**

**Tel: 0171 209 2460**

Fax: 0171 209 2461

**or STEPFAMILY HELPLINE 0171 209 2464**

For more information, see the order form at the back of this book.

# PART FOUR:
# EXTRA HELP AND INFORMATIONS

## QUICK WORD REFERENCE GUIDE

**Absent parent**
A term used by the Child Support Act to describe the parent of a qualifying child who does not have the day to day care of the child. See also *parent with care*.

**Access**
The old name for *contact*.

**Additional Voluntary Contributions (AVCs)**
A way of topping up your contributions to your company pension scheme.

**Affidavit**
A sworn written statement. See also *exhibit*.

**Ancillary relief**
The general term for court orders relating to property or financial matters in divorce or judicial separation proceedings.

**Annuity**
A regular payment made for the rest of your life. Depending on its terms it or part of it may pass onto your partner after your death.

**Answer**
The respondent's defence to a divorce petition in which they deny the allegations or cross petition.

**Barrister**
A specialist lawyer and adviser to a solicitor. A barrister may represent you in court.

**Basic rate tax**
The middle rate of tax. For 1995/6 the rate is 25 per cent. This is charged on all taxable income between £3200 and £24,300. This

in turn is known as the basic rate tax band. The basic rate is also used, by for example, banks and building societies, to deduct tax at source on some savings accounts.

**Beneficiary**
Someone who has the right to something under the terms of a will or an investment policy.

**Capital Gains Tax (CGT)**
A tax on the sale of assets such as shares, land or antiques.

**Care and control**
An obsolete term which used to describe the responsibility of looking after a child's day to day needs.

**Child of the family**
Any child of husband or wife or both who has been treated as a child of the family. This excludes foster children.

**Clean break**
A once and for all divorce settlement. The terms cannot be varied after the order is made even if circumstances change. However, the CSA may be able to override such agreements made after April 1993 with regard to maintenance for children.

**Conciliation and mediation**
The involvement of mediators to help couples reach agreement on issues such as money and arrangements for the children. Not to be confused with reconciliation.

**Consent order**
Court order made on terms agreed by both husband and wife.

## Contact

New name for access. An order made under the Children Act to enable a child to have contact with the parent or any other named adult with whom the child does not live.

## Contracted-out (pension schemes)

Employer's pension which has been certified by the government as providing benefits equivalent to SERPS. As a result employees pay reduced National Insurance Contributions but don't get SERPS. The opposite, of course, is a contracted-in pension scheme.

## Counsel

Another name for a *barrister*.

## Custody

The old term for *residence orders*.

## Decree absolute

The final order that dissolves a marriage.

## Decree nisi

The interim order issued once the courts are satisfied that grounds for divorce have been established.

## Defined benefit schemes

See *final salary pension schemes*.

## Defined contribution schemes

See *money purchase schemes*.

## Deposit-based pensions

A pension where your money is invested in a deposit account.

## Disclosure

Providing all the information that is required, for example in court.

## District judge

Formerly known as a registrar. Usually a former solicitor who is appointed to deal with a wide range of court matters including those related to divorce.

## Dividend

Income from shares.

## Domicile

A legal concept meaning – in the broadest terms – the country which someone regards as their permanent home either through birth or choice of residence.

## Endowment policies

A long-term investment with a life assurance attached.

## Equity (of a property)

The net worth of a home after the mortgage and any other associated debts are repaid and the expenses of the sale met.

## Executors

People who administer a will.

## Exhibit

A document referred to in, and sworn with, an *affidavit*.

## Ex parte

An application to the court without having notified the other person involved.

## Filing

Presenting or sending documents to the court. For example, filing a divorce petition.

## Final salary pension schemes

A type of company pension scheme that pays you a percentage of your final year's salary which increases annually in line with inflation.

## Free-standing additional voluntary contributions (FSAVCs)

Money from your earnings which you can pay into a pension plan which is outside your company's pension scheme.

## Friendly societies

Similar to a building society, these are small insurance companies owned by their members and run for the benefit of those members as opposed to outside shareholders.

**Gilts**
Government securities. The means by which the government borrows money through the stock market.

**Green form**
Popular term for initial advice under the legal aid scheme.

**Gross**
The total amount of income or money before any deductions such as tax or expenses are taken off. As opposed to *net*.

**Higher rate tax**
Tax paid at a higher rate, currently 40 per cent on all taxable income over the upper limit of the *basic rate tax* band.

**Independent financial advisers**
People who can give independent advice on the best forms of savings and investments for you. They are not tied to any particular product or service provider and they must be authorised to practise.

**Indexation allowance**
An allowance against *capital gains tax* to take account of inflation.

**Inheritance Act**
The law which allows certain people to make a claim on an estate if they feel they have been inadequately provided for under the terms of a will.

**Inheritance tax**
A tax on gifts. Despite its name it can be paid on gifts made during your lifetime as well as those you make on your death through your will or under the intestacy rules.

**Injunction**
A court order telling someone to do, or not to do something. The penalty for breaking the terms of an injunction can be imprisonment.

**Intestacy rules**
The laws which state how an estate can be divided up when someone dies without making a will.

**Intestate**
When you die without making a will.

**Investment trust**
A company which in turn invests in other companies.

**Legacies**
Specific gifts left in a will.

**Legal Aid**
Government-aided means-tested scheme to provide legal advice and help for those unable to pay.

**Letters of administration**
A court order used instead of *probate* where there is no will.

**Money purchase schemes**
A type of company pension. They don't guarantee a fixed income but invest your contributions in a fund which buys an *annuity* when you retire.

**National savings**
A variety of savings schemes by which the government raises money. Available through the Post Office.

**Net**
The amount of money or savings left after, for example, tax has been deducted.

**Net of tax**
The amount of income received after tax has been deducted at source, in other words before you get it.

**Ombudsman**
The person to whom you can take an unresolved complaint to see if it can be resolved. You may also be able to receive compensation. Their services are free. Many professions and services in the financial sector are regulated by an ombudsman.

## Open market option

The opportunity to move a mature personal pension to another insurance company.

## Parental responsibility

The rights and duties parents have towards their children. Mothers and married fathers automatically have parental responsibility, while unmarried fathers can acquire it as well as other people, for example guardians and step-parents, through for example a residence order.

## Parent with care

Term used by the Child Support Agency to describe the parent with whom a child lives and who has day-to-day responsibility for the child.

## PAYE

Pay As You Earn. The way most employees pay their tax. Tax is deducted by your employer before you receive your wages.

## Pensionable employment

A job that gives you the option to join a company's pension scheme.

## Personal Equity Plans

A tax-free way of investing limited amounts of money in shares, units or investment trusts.

## Portability

The option to move your pension scheme if you change jobs. With fully portable schemes there is no financial penalty.

## Potentially Exempt Transfer (PET)

An exemption from *inheritance tax* for many lifetime gifts.

## Probate

Authorisation from the court enabling an *executor* to dispose of an asset according to the terms of a will.

## Qualifying child

Term laid down by the Child Support Act which means a child under 16 or under 19 and in full-time advanced education, one of whose parents is an *absent parent*.

## Residence order

An order which states where a child shall live.

## SERPS

The State Earnings Related Pension Scheme. An additional State pension linked to your earnings which is paid with the basic retirement pension. It is paid for through National Insurance contributions.

## Shares or equities

A fixed division of a company's capital. Each share can be sold – and resold. Its value will depend on the state of the market and on how well the company performs.

## Statutory charge

Anyone receiving *legal aid* may have to repay some or all of their legal costs if they gain or retain any money or property in the course of the legal proceedings.

## Summons

A demand issued by the court for someone to appear in court at a specified time.

## Tax allowances

The amount of income you are allowed to earn or receive before you have to start paying income tax.

## Tax relief

Certain payments and items such as losses or essential equipment that can be set against your income and help reduce your tax liabilities.

## Taxed at source

Income from investments which has had tax deducted from it before you receive it.

## Tied agents

Financial advisers who are tied to one financial service company. They can only recommend products supplied by that company.

## Unit-linked

Can be applied to any investment like a pension or life assurance plan. It simply means being invested in units in an investment fund, the value of which will rise and fall according to changes in the stock market.

## Unit trusts

A fund of money pooled between investors which is used to buy shares in a range of companies. The fund is divided into equal portions or units whose value rises or falls depending on the performance of the underlying investments.

## Without prejudice

A phrase which is used to prevent, for example, a letter used in negotiations from being used as evidence in court if the negotiations fail to be settled out of court.

## With-profits pensions

Personal pension schemes which pay an annual bonus out of the profits the fund earns.

# RESOURCE LIST

This section contains contact details for organisations which may be able to give advice and help to stepfamilies, some of which have already been mentioned in this book.

It is worth remembering that organisations, particularly voluntary organisations, do change addresses and telephone numbers. The details given here are as up to date as possible, but if you are unable to contact a particular organisation you may need to ring Directory Enquiries or try another, similar group to see if they have the new details. Also many voluntary organisations often have small numbers of staff who work only for limited periods, so you may have to call a number of times or leave a message on an answering machine.

Some organisations may have local or regional offices – look in your telephone directory.

## General Advice

**National Association of
Citizens Advice Bureaux,**
Myddelton House,
115-123 Pentonville Road,
London N1 9LZ
Tel: 0171 833 2181
Citizens Advice Bureaux can give a wide range of information and advice about consumer, legal and benefit issues. Consult your telephone directory or ring the national office for details of your nearest bureau.

**National Council for Voluntary Organisations**
(NCVO), Regent's Wharf,
8 All Saints Street,
London, N1 9RL
Tel: 0171 713 6161
Can provide details of voluntary, charitable and self-help groups.

# Children

## Association of Lawyers for Children,
for *membership and general enquiries contact*
Jeremy Bartley, Ronald Prior & Co,
165-167 Hoe Street, Walthamstow,
London, E17 3AL
Tel: 0181 520 8632
Fax: 0181 509 0237
*for the newsletter contact*
Barbara Mitchels
Point House, 42 Yarmouth Road, Thorpe St Andrew,
Norwich, NR7 0EQ
Tel: 01603 300 425

## Child Abduction Unit,
Official Solicitors Department,
81 Chancery Lane, London, WC2A 1DD
Tel: 0171 911 7127

## Child Poverty Action Group,
1-5 Bath Street, London, EC1V 9PY
Tel: 0171 253 3406

## Child Support Agency,
24th Floor, Millbank Tower,
21-24 Millbank, London, SW1 4QU
Tel: 0171 217 4789
Tel: National Enquiry Line: 0345 133 133
Tel: Employers' Enquiry Line: 0345 134 134
Tel: Child Support Literature Line: 0345 830 830

## Children's Legal Centre,
University of Essex
Wivenhoe Park, Colchester, Essex CO4 3SQ
Tel: 01206 873820

## Families Need Fathers
(National Administration Centre),
134 Curtain Road, London, EC2A 3AR
Tel: 0171 613 5060

## Mothers Apart From Their Children (MATCH),
c/o BM Problems, London,
WC1N 3XX

# Counselling

**Asian Family Counselling Service,**
74 The Avenue, West Ealing, London, W13 8LB
Tel: 0181 997 5749

**Care Marriage,**
23 Kensington Square, London W8 5HN
or Clitheroe House, 1 Blythe Mews,
Blythe Road, London, W14 0NW
Tel: 0171 937 3781
and 0171 371 1341
A marriage advisory service for Catholics.

**Cruse Bereavement Care,**
Cruse House, 126 Sheen Road,
Richmond, Surrey, TW9 1UR
Tel: 0181 940 4818
Helpline: 0181 332 7227 (Mon–Fri, 9.30 am–5 pm)

**Institute of Family Therapy,**
43 New Cavendish Street, London, W1M 7RG
Tel: 0171 935 1651
Offers therapy to families who are experiencing
relationship, psychological and behavioural
difficulties.

**Jewish Marriage Council,**
23 Ravenshurst Avenue, London, NW4 4EE
Tel: 0181 203 6311
Advice: 0181 203 6314
Helpline: 0345 581999

**London Marriage Guidance Council,**
76a New Cavendish Street, Corner of Harley Street,
London, W1M 7LB
Tel: 0171 580 1087

**RELATE, Marriage Guidance,**
Herbert Gray College, Little Church Street, Rugby,
Warwickshire, CV21 3AP
Tel: 01788 573 241
Fax: 01788 535 007
RELATE offers a wide range of services and has local
branches – consult your telephone directory.

## Mediation

**National Family Mediation,**
9 Tavistock Place, London, WC1H 9SN
Tel: 0171 383 5993
Fax: 0171 383 5994
An umbrella organisation which can put you in touch
with local services.

**Family Mediators Association,**
PO Box 2028, Hove, East Sussex, BN3 3HU
Tel: 01273 747 750

**Family Mediation Scotland,**
127 Rose Street, South Lane, Edinburgh, EH2 4BB
Tel: 0131 220 1610

## Families

**Family Rights Group (England & Wales),**
The Print House, 18 Ashwin Street, London, E8 3DL
Advice line: 0171 249 0008
(every weekday, 1.30 pm–3 pm)

**Gingerbread,**
16-17 Clerkenwell Close, London, EC1R 0AA
England advice line: 0171 336 8184
Wales advice line: 01792 648728

**Gingerbread Scotland,**
The Mary Hill Community Central Hall,
304 Mary Hill Road, Glasgow, G20 7YE
Tel: 0141 353 0989

**National Association of Widows,**
54–57 Allison Street, Digbeth, Birmingham,
West Midlands, B5 5TH
Tel: 0121 643 8348

**National Council for the Divorced and Separated,**
13 High Street, Little Shelford,
Cambridgeshire, CB2 5ES
Tel: 0116 270 0595

**National Council for One Parent Families,**
255 Kentish Town Road, London, NW5 2LX
Tel: 0171 267 1361

**National Stepfamily Association,**
3rd Floor, Chapel House, 18 Hatton Place,
London, EC1N 8RU
Tel: 0171 209 2460
Helpline: 0171 209 2464

**One Parent Families Scotland,**
13 Gayfield Square, Edinburgh, EH1 3NX
Tel: 0131 556 3899

**Stepfamily Scotland,**
22 Chalmers Street, Dunfermline, Fife, KY12 8AT
Tel: 01383 622197

**Soldiers' Sailors' and Airmen's Families
Association (SSAFA),**
19 Queen Elizabeth Street, London, SE1 2LP
Tel: 0171 403 8783

**Women's Aid Federation,**
PO Box 391, Bristol, BS99 7WS
Helpline: 0117 963 3542
Gives advice and support, and temporary refuge, to
any woman in danger from physical or mental violence.

## Legal advice

**Family Law Bar Association,**
Queen Elizabeth Building, Temple,
London, EC4Y 9BS
Tel: 0171 797 7837

**Law Society,**
50-52 Chancery Lane, London, WC2A 1SX
Tel: 0171 242 1222

**Legal Action Group,**
242 Pentonville Road, London, N1 9UN
Tel: 0171 833 2931

**Legal Aid Board,**
85 Gray's Inn Road, London, WC1X 8AA
Tel: 0171 813 1000
Can supply information about the legal aid scheme.
Consult your telephone directory for your local office.

**Rights of Women,**
52–54 Featherstone Street, London, EC1Y 8RT
Tel: 0171 251 6577
Provides free legal advice to women.

**Solicitors' Family Law Association,**
PO Box 302, Orpington, Kent, BR6 8QX
Tel: 01689 850227
Will provide addresses of solicitors specialising in
family law.

## Financial advice

**National Debtline,**
Birmingham Settlement, 318 Summar Lane,
Birmingham, B19 3RL
Tel: 0121 359 8501
Provides advice to anyone with financial problems.

**Bankruptcy Association of Great Britain & Ireland,**
4 Johnson Close, Abraham Heights, Lancaster,
Lancashire, LA1 5EU
Tel: 01482 658701

**Capital Taxes Office Enquiry Team – Inheritance
Tax,**
PO Box 38, Castle Meadow Road, Notts, NG2 1BB
Tel: 0115 974 2400

**Council of Mortgage Lenders,**
3 Savile Row, London, W1X 1AF
Tel: 0171 437 0655

**Department of Social Security**
Free telephone advice service: 0800 666555

**IFA Promotions,**
4th Floor, 28 Greville Street, London EC1N 8SU
Helpline: 0171 813 4027
Will provide names and addresses of independent
financial advisers.

**Inland Revenue,**
Tax Enquiry Centres are listed in the telephone book
under Inland Revenue.

**Money Management, National Register
of Fee Based Advisors,**
Freepost 22 (SW1565), London, W1E 7EZ
Tel: 0117 976 9444
Will provide a list of fee-based financial advisers in
your area free of charge.

**Occupational Pensions Advisory Service,**
11 Belgrave Road, London, SW1V 1RB
Tel: 0171 233 8080

**ProShare Association,**
Library Chambers, 13 & 14 Basinghall Street,
London, EC2V 5BQ
Tel: 0171 600 0984
Promotes wider share ownership. Issues a Guide to
Information Sources for the Private Investor.

**Tax Aid,**
Lin Burn House, 342 Kilburn High Road,
London, NW6 2QJ
Tel: 0171 328 9521

## Other sources of advice

**Federation of Independent Advice Centres (FIAC),**
13 Stockwell Road, London, SW9 9AU
Tel: 0171 274 1839

**National Consumer Council,**
20 Grosvenor Gardens, London, SW1W 0DH
Tel: 0171 730 3469

**National Federation of Retirement Pensions
Associations (Pensioners' Voice)**
14 St Peter Street, Blackburn, Lancashire, BB2 2HD
Tel: 01254 52606

**Office of Fair Trading,**
Field House, 15–25 Breams Buildings,
London, EC4A 1PR
Tel: 0171 242 2858

# WHERE TO COMPLAIN

Mistakes can and do happen. The area of second and subsequent family financial planning is not widely recognised as needing additional and maybe sometimes different advice and information.

The first place to refer your complaint is to the organisation or adviser you are complaining about. If you are unable to agree, you can approach the regulatory body for that organisation. If still unsuccessful, you can appeal to the relevant ombudsman for a ruling, as long as you do so within certain time limits and the complaint has not been taken to court. The service is free, and an ombudsman's ruling is usually binding on the organisation concerned.

## Regulatory bodies

**Institute of Chartered Accountants in England & Wales,**
Chartered Accountants' Hall, PO Box 433,
Moorgate Place, Moorgate, London, EC2P 2BJ
Tel: 0171 920 8100
Fax: 0171 920 0547

**Insurance Brokers Registration Council,**
15 St Helens Place, London, EC3A 6DS
Tel: 0171 588 4387

**Investment Management Regulatory Organisation**
( IMRO ), Lloyd Chambers, 1 Portsoken Street,
London, E1 8BT
Tel: 0171 390 5000

**Securities and Investment Board (SIB),**
Gavrelle House, 2–14 Bunhill Row,
London, EC1Y 8RA
Tel: 0171 638 1240
The chief regulatory body for the financial services
industry, who can also tell you which body is
responsible for the financial organisation you wish
to complain about.

**Solicitors's Complaints Bureau,**
Victoria Court, 8 Dormer Place, Leamington Spa,
Warwickshire, CV32 5AE
Tel: 01926 820 082

# Ombudsmen

**Banking Ombudsman,**
70 Gray's Inn Road,
London, WC1X 8NB
Tel: 0171 404 9944

**Building Societies Ombudsman,**
Grosvenor Gardens House,
35–37 Grosvenor Gardens,
London, SW1X 7AW
Tel: 0171 931 0044

**Corporate Estate Agents Ombudsman,**
Beckett House, 4 Bridge Street,
Salisbury, Wiltshire, SP1 2LX
Tel: 01722 333 306

**Insurance Ombudsman Bureau,**
135 Park Street,
London, SE1 9EA
Tel: 0171 928 7600

**Investment Ombudsman,**
4th Floor, 6 Frederick's Place,
London, EC2R 8BT
Tel: 0171 796 3065

**Legal Services Ombudsman,**
22 Oxford Court, Oxford Street,
Manchester, M2 3WQ
Tel: 0161 236 9532

**Pensions Ombudsman,**
11 Belgrave Road,
London, SW1V 1RB
Tel: 0171 834 9144

**Personal Investment Authority
Ombudsman Bureau,**
3rd Floor, Centre Point,
103 New Oxford Street,
London, WC1A 1QH
Tel: 0171 240 3838

# USEFUL BOOKS

**Aleksander, Tobe** (1992)
*The Complete Guide To Living Together*
HEADLINE

**Aleksander, Tobe** (1995)
*Separation and Divorce:*
*A Guide for Women in Mid-life and Beyond*
AGE CONCERN

**Batchelor, Jane, Dimmock, Brian, & Smith, Donna** (1994)
*Understanding Stepfamilies: What can be learned from*
*callers to the STEPFAMILY Telephone Counselling Service*
STEPFAMILY PUBLICATIONS

**Clout, Imogen** (1993)
*Where There's a Will There's a Way: Making a will in a stepfamily*
STEPFAMILY PUBLICATIONS

**Cox, Kathleen** (1995)
*Another Step: Weddings in stepfamilies*
STEPFAMILY PUBLICATIONS

**De'Ath, Erica** (1993)
*A Baby of Our Own, A new baby in a stepfamily*
STEPFAMILY PUBLICATIONS

**De'Ath, Erica & Slater, Dee** *(Eds)* (1992)
*Parenting Threads: Caring for children when couples part*
STEPFAMILY PUBLICATIONS

**Dimmock, Brian** *(Ed.)* (1992)
*A Step In Both Directions? The impact of the Children Act*
*on Stepfamilies.* STEPFAMILY PUBLICATIONS

**Garlick, Helen** (1992)
*The Which? Guide To Divorce: The essential practical guide to*
*the legal and financial arrangements for divorce,*
CONSUMER'S ASSOCIATION/HODDER & STOUGHTON

**Garnhan, A & Knights, E** (1994)
*Child Support Handbook, 1994/95* Second Edition
CHILD POVERTY ACTION GROUP

**Street, M** (1994)
*Money and Family Breakdown, 1994/95*
*The practitioners guide to benefits and child support,*
Second Edition

# INDEX

## For further information, advice and support about stepfamily matters you can contact:

STEPFAMILY,
Chapel House, 18 Hatton Place,
London EC1N 8RU

Tel: 0171 209 2460

Fax: 0171 209 2461

or STEPFAMILY HELPLINE 0171 209 2464

### Ways in which you can give

**Bankers Order:** a regular payment, even £10 a month, helps keep our services going.

**Give As You Earn:** if your employer has a Give As You Earn scheme you can make a monthly donation before tax is deducted and cut down your tax bill.

**Gift Aid:** a donation of £250 or more by Gift Aid is worth more to us as we can claim the tax already paid.

**Legacy:** If you would like to make such a gift through a legacy in your will or to add a codicil to your existing will we suggest you go to your solicitor who will be happy to advise you.

### Please send me details of

☐ STEPFAMILY membership

☐ other publications – leaflets and books

☐ how to become a volunteer telephone counsellor

☐ more information on donating to STEPFAMILY

Name

Address

Postcode

Return this form to: STEPFAMILY,
Chapel House, 18 Hatton Place, London, EC1N 8RU

Registered Charity No. 1005351 Company No. 2552166

ORDER FORM OVERLEAF

# ORDER FORM

Please indicate which book(s) you are ordering,
how many copies and circle the price

| | Price | Mem | Cost |
|---|---|---|---|
| Adopting Stepchildren (pk 10) | £5.00 | £5.00 | |
| A Step in Both Directions | £7.50 | £6.50 | |
| A Baby of our own | £4.00 | £4.00 | |
| Changing families | £4.50 | £4.00 | |
| Children & Divorce | £5.00 | £3.00 | |
| Dinosaurs Divorce | £3.99 | | |
| Fact File no. 1 / 2 / 3 | £2.00 | £1.50 | |
| Set of 3 | £5.00 | £4.00 | |
| Parenting Threads | £4.00 | £3.40 | |
| Reading List ch/par | £0.75 | £0.50 | |
| Set of 3 (incl prof) | £2.50 | £1.50 | |
| Stepfamilies | £11.00 | £9.35 | |
| Stepfamilies and Adoption | £3.00 | £2.55 | |
| Step by Step | £10.95 | £9.30 | |
| Stepfamilies Talking | £4.00 | £3.40 | |
| Stepfathering | £4.00 | £3.40 | |
| Stepmothering | £9.95 | £8.45 | |
| Stepping Out | £3.50 | | |
| Step-parenting | £2.50 | £2.10 | |
| Teenagers | £1.20 | £1.00 | |
| To & Fro Children | £6.99 | | |
| Understanding Stepfamilies | £9.50 | £8.00 | |
| Where there's a Will | £4.00 | £3.40 | |
| Post & Packing | | | |
| Total | | | |

P&P costs: 50p for under £5.00, £1 for £5 or over, £2.00 for £15 or over
( Overseas orders will be invoiced for actual postage costs)

**Please make cheque/postal order (in £ Sterling)
payable to STEPFAMILY**

National Stepfamily Association
Chapel House, 18 Hatton Place, London  EC1N 8RU
Tel: 0171 209 2460   Fax: 0171 209 2461
Counselling: 0171 209 2464

Registered Charity No. 1005351 Company limited by Guarantee 2552166